HOW TO BE
GOOD

THE STRUGGLE BETWEEN LAW & ETHICS

ALSO BY PHILIP SLAYTON

Lawyers Gone Bad: Money, Sex and Madness
in Canada's Legal Profession (2007)

Mighty Judgment: How the Supreme Court
of Canada Runs Your Life (2011)

Bay Street: A Novel (2013)

Mayors Gone Bad (2015)

HOW TO BE
GOOD

THE STRUGGLE BETWEEN LAW & ETHICS

PHILIP SLAYTON
with PATRICIA CHISOLM

Oblonsky Editions

HOW TO BE GOOD: THE STRUGGLE BETWEEN LAW AND ETHICS

Published by Oblonsky Editions, Toronto, Canada

First published 2017

Copyright © Philip Slayton and Patricia Chisholm, 2017

ISBN: 978-0-9936389-7-8

Project management by Gabrielle Domingues for Oblonsky Editions.
Cover design by Brian Halley of Right Think.
Interior design by 52 Novels.

Dedicated to
Michael Fitz-James (1951 – 2005)

TABLE OF CONTENTS

FOREWORD
BY JULIAN PORTER, Q.C

Julian Porter is one of Canada's most distinguished barristers. He is a bencher of the Law Society of Upper Canada and has been awarded an honorary LL.D. by Queen's University. Julian Porter has written two books of art criticism.

Philip Slayton's career reveals someone comfortable in a wide range of different — and demanding — roles, even by the standards of the legal profession. Rhodes Scholar, clerk to a Justice of the Supreme Court of Canada, dean at Western University's Faculty of Law at age 34, commercial lawyer for a prominent Toronto law firm for 17 years and now a successful author and past President of PEN Canada, a position that requires courage as well as commitment.

I read many of these columns when they were first published, and they often made me bridle; I felt some were either unfair, or the solutions offered impractical, or both. Now, reading them in sequence and with the benefit of greater perspective, I find them an absolute marvel (or as he might say "bloody marvellous").

Take the intertwined issues of politics, the rule of law and access to justice: in proposing a "judicare" system, akin to "medicare", citing another's observation, he notes that, "Justice is open to all — like the Ritz Hotel." That brings all of my usual bafflegab on the point to a halt. And discussing how many of us have learned to live with this shameful gap, which leaves so many without access to justice, he says: "Sometimes we pretend otherwise but that is a *lebenslüge*, a delusion that allows us to live." I never heard the word until now, but it certainly fits.

He writes of the crippling ailment of depression, which burdens so many lawyers, partly due to the practice of law degenerating into a pure business, with little thought for the social ends and rebalancing of rights it should also entail. Coming out of that fog, and the hope that can follow, he enlists the help of Dante: "Thence we came forth to re-behold its stars". Any writer that ends a column with that can't be all bad.

He is critical of billing by the hour (rightfully so) which, he says, leads to a lead foot and heavy hand. In yet another compact but decisive dismissal of the opposing side, he writes: "This approach would value a painting by Picasso according to how long it had taken him to paint it."

This work will educate in the great sense: it forces you to examine the frailties of a supposedly special — even idealistic — profession, with the work of lawyers sold as a benefit and a necessity for the good of others. But it doesn't hurt to emphasize its failings. We must never ignore them. He and Ms. Chisholm do an essential job of poking us hard. I am the better for it and so shall you be.

And we should read it again in five years to see if we've learned from and listened to these important observations about our too often overlooked imperfections, especially his advice to young lawyers. His road map for a new lawyer is startling, including a central piece of advice: don't work too hard. You will ask, "What kind of advice is that?" Well, after more than 50 years of being a barrister I would say it's good advice. Working too hard leads to being a workaholic, a disease difficult to shed.

Read widely, he advises: "You enlarge what you know and understand by reading — history, biography, philosophy. Sometimes fiction is the best thing to read because fiction unlocks the human heart unlike anything else."

I believe Mr. Slayton's advice is vital. Sometimes it will sideswipe you but you will also find a refuge, a strength, and the knowledge that you are not alone. Your developing sensitivity will be a passport to a complete life. Read as if your life depends on it. After five years, make sure you look at his instructions and count how many of his markers you've accomplished. Do it and you'll be better for it.

INTRODUCTION

Michael Fitz-James called me in the summer of 2002. He'd been a student of mine at McGill University's law school in the 1970s. We hadn't kept in touch but remembered each other. Now he was editor of the magazine *Canadian Lawyer*. He'd noticed a series of articles I'd written for *The Globe and Mail*. "How'd you like to write some stuff for me?" he asked. I agreed. Why not? It was two years since I'd left a Bay Street law practice and I had time on my hands.

Thus began my long relationship with *Canadian Lawyer* that has now encompassed five editors. I've written about 150 articles for the magazine, some 200,000 words. Fifty or so columns have been on problems of legal ethics. This book is a collection of those particular pieces. It is dedicated to Michael Fitz-James who died of Lou Gehrig's Disease in 2005. Michael was a pioneer legal journalist, excelling at the popular interpretation of law-related events for both lawyers and non-lawyers. He was a big personality, and ferociously funny.

Michael was succeeded as editor of *Canadian Lawyer* by lawyer/journalist Patricia Chisholm, who selected the columns in this book, organized them thematically, and wrote the brief introductions that give a contemporary context. Before she became editor of *Canadian Lawyer* Patricia spent more than a decade as a writer and editor at

Maclean's magazine. She now focuses on law- and- finance related journalism. I am seriously indebted to her for her help and advice.

The columns are largely unchanged from the ones that appeared in the magazine (the dates given are when the columns were written; typically they were published the following month). There are a few minor stylistic changes for the sake of uniformity. I have added an occasional footnote where some updating seemed necessary. And I have taken the opportunity to correct some spelling and grammatical mistakes.

A NOTE ON TERMS

While these columns try to avoid legal jargon, a few arcane terms creep in from time-to-time.

One is "law society." This refers to the self-regulatory bodies that are responsible for the professional supervision of lawyers in Canada. The term derives from English practice. One province, Ontario, still uses the name given to their society prior to Confederation: The Law Society of Upper Canada (although a proposal is current to change the name to The Law Society of Ontario — let's hope it succeeds).

The authority of these societies is delegated to them by provincial legislatures and they are administered by lawyers called "benchers" elected by members of the profession. The law societies make and enforce the rules of professional conduct that lawyers must abide by: matters they rule on can range from the handling of client trust funds to the correct course of action when a lawyer knows a client is lying. The law societies are also responsible for the professional discipline of lawyers, including the power to hold hearings investigating their conduct and the power to expel them from the profession.

"*Charter*" is a word that appears in many of the columns. This refers to the Canadian *Charter of Rights and Freedoms*, a constitutional document enacted in 1982. It codifies several categories of individual rights and fundamental freedoms, such as freedom of expression, and restricts the power of the state to abrogate these rights, except in a limited number of circumstances. It has been heavily relied upon by litigants seeking redress from state action since it was put into force and now forms a fundamental element of the Canadian legal system.

LAW IN A MORAL VACUUM

THE GENDER GAP
NOVEMBER 2016

"It's a big ethical issue if women are disadvantaged, simply because they are women." *On November 8, 2016 Hillary Clinton, the Democratic nominee for President of the United States, former Senator, Secretary of State and apparent front runner throughout most of the campaign, conceded victory to the never-before elected Republican, Donald Trump. While the causes of the surprise upset will be debated for years, one important factor appears to have been Clinton's gender.*

How does the Canadian legal profession treat women lawyers? They should have exactly the same opportunities as men lawyers. But do they? It's hard to be precise about this. The data is spotty and a lot of it is out-of-date. Much of the evidence is anecdotal. But one thing's for sure: It's a big ethical problem if women are disadvantaged simply because they are women.

When I was a kid in the 1950s, growing up in a middle class area of Winnipeg, most of my friends' mothers stayed home and tended house. If a woman went out to work, it was generally because her husband had trouble making a living (or at least, that's what the local gossips said over the garden fence). There were notable exceptions, of course. People remarked on these exceptions, not always with approval.

It seems different now. Canadian women are CEOs, sit on corporate boards, are ministers of the crown. Four of the nine Supreme Court of Canada judges are female. Some say women are eclipsing men in the workplace (and elsewhere). A recent popular book was entitled *The End of Men*. In 2013, participants in Toronto's Munk Debate argued over the topic, "Be it resolved men are obsolete…"

There's a lot of hand waving about gender equality, but what's the truth of the matter? Start poking around and suddenly things don't look so great. In April 2016 it was reported by Catalyst, a not-for-profit organization that tries to expand opportunities for women, that there was just one female CEO in the TSX60, a group of 60 large Canadian companies (she's Dawn Farrell of TransAlta Corporation). In 2014, women's share of board seats in the TSX60 was 20.8 per cent. Only 26 per cent of federal MPs are women (and that's a record number). In 2015, the World Economic Forum ranked Canada #30 when it came to the status of women, down from #19 the year before (a growing wage gap was part of the explanation for the downgrade).

And what about women lawyers? The good news, first of all, is that there are a lot of them, and the number and percentage are increasing. Catalyst reports that across Canada there are now more new women lawyers than men. It's a far cry from the days, not so long ago, when a woman in a law school class or a courtroom was an oddity.

But the story of women in law does not end with the call to the bar. Many more women than men leave legal practice, often early on in their career. About ten years ago the Law Society of Upper Canada, alarmed by this trend, created something called the Retention of Women in Private Practice Working Group. The Working Group noted that retention was a problem largely because private practice has not adapted to women's realities, e.g. childbirth. The Group commissioned a change of status study of the three-year period 2010 to 2012, and found that during those years more women than men, particularly those five to nine years from their call to the bar, had left private practice and not returned. A 2016 study by the Criminal Lawyers Association found that women were leaving the practice of criminal law because (they said) of low pay, lack of financial support for maternity leave and because they were treated with less respect than men by judges and court staff. Formal studies aside, there's lots of anecdotal evidence of woman lawyers not being taken seriously enough, particularly in larger firms. There's that damn glass ceiling, although periodically a female managing partner here, or a female chief of research there, is cynically trotted out and dusted off to try and demonstrate that the glass ceiling doesn't exist.

Recent studies in the United States draw depressing conclusions about the place of women in the American legal profession. A 2016 study of partner compensation by a major U.S. legal search firm reported a 44 per cent difference in pay between female and male partners at big American law firms, apparently because men are better than women at getting credit for bringing in new clients (bringing in new clients used to be called "rainmaking" but now has the far more impressive *faux*-scientific moniker "origination"). By the way, is it true that men are betters "originators" than women, and, if so, why on earth is that the case? A 2016 survey by the New York City Bar Association, again of larger law firms, found that fewer women were working as associates than in previous years, and that firm partnerships remained more than 75 per cent white male. *The New York Times* reported, "The survey findings concluded that progress for women and minorities is hampered by high rates of lawyers leaving firms for varied reasons. Failure to attain equity, or owner, partnership — or the lack of prospects to become partner — appeared to have a significant effect on firm longevity."

I can't find any recent Canadian income studies comparable in scope to the American ones. There's the occasional analysis, here and there. A 2010 study commissioned by the Law Society of Upper Canada reported: "Women and especially visible minority lawyers earn less than their white male counterparts. Relative to men, the earnings of women lawyers increased substantially between 1970 and 1995, but there has been little improvement since. At the start of their careers the earnings of women and men are very similar, but a gender gap opens up at the age of 30 and its size increases with age." A 2015 study of junior lawyers by Ronit Dinovitzer, a University of Toronto sociologist, found that, on average, second-year male lawyers make $5,500 more than their female counterparts. For years, surveys have shown that Canadian female in-house counsel make less than their male counterparts.

I don't think we need more studies. We know something is not right. There's a big ethical problem, deeply buried in society and reflected in the legal profession. Something needs to be done. But what?

YOU CAN'T TRUST ANYONE
JUNE 2015

"The more legalistic society becomes, the less cohesive it is."
While commercial agreements, financial regulation, privacy, and
many other things, seem to be more and more heavily lawyered
with every passing year, there doesn't appear to be matching
improvement in the conduct of either individuals or corporations.

Trust and law. The optimal relationship between the two is an ethical
conundrum at the heart of legal practice. How much can we trust
each other? How much law do we need? Do unnecessary legal rules
replace trust to the detriment of a truly civil society? Does increasing legalization — turning every problem, no matter what it is really
about, into a legal issue — damage the fabric of our community?

When I practised law, I spent a lot of time drawing up contracts
for my clients and reviewing draft agreements concocted by lawyers
for the other side. There were endless meetings at which every word
of lengthy documents was anxiously analyzed and fought over by
hyper-caffeinated attorneys. Clients, eager to get on with drilling for
oil or developing real estate, often lost patience with this process,
and gave instructions to "speed it up" and "get on with the job." You
had to be tough with them, resolute, adamant, brook no nonsense,
explain how important every word was, and how they had to be
protected eight ways to Sunday from the unscrupulous folks across
the table, and how this took time, effort and skill (yours), damn the

billable hours, full steam ahead. Remember, you'd tell them, a well-drafted agreement is your best protection. Don't forget, *you can't trust anyone.*

Then, one sunny day, I retired from legal practice. After messing about for a bit, I decided to become an author. Why not? (Although, it's easier said than done: as one literary friend said to me, "it's hard to write even a bad book.") In due course, a big publishing house presented me with a book contract. Without bothering to read it, I signed on the dotted line. I couldn't be bothered to wade through a bunch of complicated provisions. They didn't matter. I wanted to sell my book. And, I liked the person on the other side of the table. More than that: I trusted her. If there were any difficulties down the road (and occasionally there were), I was confident that good faith conversations would fix them (they did). I don't remember if we shook hands, but we might as well have done. *I relied on trust.*

Ah hah, the reader of this column may be thinking, I get it! You believe that you're better off signing a contract without reading it, particularly if you're a little guy dealing with a big corporation which puts a "take it or leave it" standard form agreement on the table. You can always claim later you didn't know what you were doing, you didn't understand what was happening, the offensive provision in question can't possibly be binding, you didn't have a choice, you were being pushed around and you didn't even realize it, inequality of bargaining power, etc., etc. That sort of argument might work for some people — I'm not sure if it would today, Lord Denning's been dead a long time — but I don't think it would apply to me, given how I earned my living for many years.

My change of attitude once I left legal practice got me thinking about the relationship between trust and law. It's clearly inverse. The less we trust each other, the more we rely on rules. That's true in private law, regulating dealings between people, and it's true in public law, governing the relationship between citizens and the state. If I'm doing business with someone I don't trust, I want a comprehensive, ironclad, enforceable contract. If the state is suspicious of its citizens, it will increase surveillance and limit freedom of expression. It will legislate *An Act to enact the Security of Canada Information Sharing*

Act and the Secure Air Travel Act, to amend the Criminal Code, the Canadian Security Intelligence Service Act and the Immigration and Refugee Protection Act and to make related and consequential amendments to other Acts (to give Bill C-51 its full, and frightening, name. It's colloquially known as the "Anti-terrorism Act" and was passed in 2015.)

Obviously a complex society like Canada, containing people with diverse interests and ambitions, and different cultural backgrounds and aspirations, cannot run on trust alone. We must have a framework of private and public law to regulate and resolve inevitable conflict. And the relationship between trust and law is intricate. Fair rules, fairly applied, stimulate trust. Living in a law-abiding society, provided it has the right laws and there are not too many of them, is reassuring. Ronald Reagan was on to something when (in the context of strategic arms limitation negotiations), he said, "trust, but verify." The trick is to find the right balance between trust and verification, between trust and law.

I think that society is better off erring on the trust side of the equation. The more it relies on trust, the healthier it is, and the healthier it will become. A handshake is better than a written agreement. Why do I say this? There is no set of neat arguments in favour of the proposition. They should not be necessary. The proposition is self-evident. It is a mistake always to be filling in perceived, and perhaps imaginary, gaps in the social structure with complicated law. The more legalistic society becomes, the less cohesive it is. Eventually it will collapse, topple over, from its own legal weight.

For obvious reasons, many lawyers find this point of view hard to accept. Here is an ethical dilemma at the heart of the profession. A lawyer's job is to lay on the law. His job is to reduce problems and disputes, some with deep and complex origins, to neat legal issues that can be resolved — maybe — by a ponderous and expensive legal mechanism available only to the rich and near rich. He works for an individual, a person or a corporation, in an adversary system. But, arguably, none of this benefits the broader community; indeed, it may be damaging. It's a profoundly worrying thought for members of the legal profession. Or should be.

LAWYER AS GURU
JUNE 2013

"Issues once considered social or political or philosophical are now holus-bolus regarded as legal." In May 2013 then Toronto Mayor Rob Ford faced allegations that he had smoked crack cocaine. He remained silent, on the advice of his lawyers. That strategy fatally undermined his credibility, and spelled the end of his ability to guide city policy.

If you win a Nobel Prize for, say, chemistry, suddenly everyone wants your views on, I don't know what, maybe world peace. Why being a whiz at infrared chemiluminescence makes you an expert on nuclear disarmament is not clear but — such is the undifferentiated prestige of a Nobel — apparently it does.

Being a lawyer is a bit like that, in a much smaller way of course. If you're a lawyer, people seek out your advice at cocktail parties about whether their pesky Uncle Fred should be put in a nursing home or if renting an apartment is better than buying a condominium, apparently believing these problems may have tricky legal implications. They want your opinion on this stuff *because you're a lawyer*. It doesn't matter to them that studying *Rylands v. Fletcher* twenty years ago only qualifies you to give advice about what happens if a reservoir bursts.

Part of the explanation for the lawyer mystique is that issues once considered social or political or philosophical are now holus-bolus regarded as legal. This has certainly been true in Canada since enactment of the *Charter* in 1982. Few would have believed 40 years ago that judges rather than elected politicians would in the future decide questions like whether running a brothel should be against the law or if it's okay to help someone commit suicide. Once every problem is characterized as a legal problem, we turn to lawyers whenever there's trouble, any kind of trouble. Lawyers have become the universal problem-solvers.

The lawyer mystique is particularly prevalent in politics. It's not because many politicians and political staffers are lawyers (43 out of 308 federal MPs, for example), although that doesn't help. It's because when politicians get into trouble, no matter what kind of trouble, they inevitably turn to lawyers for advice. It doesn't seem to matter that what is being asked for is often not legal advice at all.

What should a lawyer do in these circumstances? The answer is, have a deep sense of the limits of his expertise, and know when a question is a legal question that he can answer and when it is a non-legal question he should stay away from. To stumble around blindly is dangerous. To go beyond expertise is unethical. Would a corporate tax specialist, who'd done nothing else for years, properly give advice on, say, *Charter* rights? Of course not.

There's a recent, delicious example. Step up Mayor Rob Ford, chief magistrate of the great city of Toronto! When the allegations that Mayor Ford had smoked crack first surfaced, around the middle of May, Ford said nothing for a week. Asked about Ford's silence, Toronto deputy mayor Doug Holyday said, "The only thing I've been able to get from him and some people on his staff is, I guess, that the lawyers that they are dealing with suggest the less they say at this point, the better." Eventually, Ford himself said, "for the past week, on the advice of my solicitors, I was advised not to say a word."

But saying nothing was a disastrous strategy for Ford. His silence fuelled speculation, suspicion, rumour, and ridicule. If he was acting on the advice of lawyers, he got very bad advice. If what we read in the newspapers is true, "the lawyers" treated the situation as a legal problem rather than a political crisis. That was a big and clumsy mistake. A political crisis needs to be handled quite differently from a legal problem.

My friend Steven Skurka, host of *Closing Arguments* on NewsTalk 1010 (full disclosure: I've been a guest on his show several times), doesn't agree. He has written in the *Huffington Post*, "in general terms, lawyers instruct their clients to be vigilant and keep quiet about their matter for one principle reason; it could harm their case or legal position." Skurka continues: "It was, in reality, a measured and not a capricious decision. Rob Ford's lawyer is deserving of no blame." But in the same article, Skurka admits that there was no conceivable chance of Ford being criminally charged. The point is, there was no "case" and there was no "legal position," and it was seriously misguided to behave as if there were.

It's always amusing when some public figure doesn't show up for an unpleasant event citing "doctor's orders." Pseudo-legal advice can be used in the same way as phony medical commands. Sometimes the charade is not entirely the lawyer's fault. If a powerful client demands legal advice that he can hide behind, it may be hard to resist. So out it comes: "I'd love to help you/answer your question/assist in the inquiry, but my lawyer has instructed me not to."

Everyone who has practised law has run into this problem. The equivalent in the world of corporate law is a formal legal opinion seeking to justify some less-than-savoury transaction. Who can resist the powerful and wealthy client? But the ethics of the situation are clear. Legal advice and opinions should not be for sale — at least, not in this way.

What about the lawyer whose advice is sought about all kinds of different things, not because of his legal expertise so much, but because of his well-known general sagacity and extraordinarily broad experience? Most of us know someone like that — the lawyer who acts as a trusted long-time family adviser, or a CEO's right-hand man, or a *consigliere*. This particular lawyer isn't ethically restricted in the way I've described, provided it's explicit that he's not being asked for legal advice and he's not giving it, and provided his advice is not misrepresented as a legal opinion. Those provisos seem obvious, but, oh, how many times they are ignored!

The Bible says it all: "Whoever walks with the wise becomes wise, but the companion of fools will suffer harm." (Proverbs 13:20)

WHEN POLICING IS WORSE THAN THE CRIME
AUGUST 2012

"Two crazy proceedings, both damaging to the justice system. Save us from the disciplinarians." Long-running reviews by the legal profession of the conduct of two lawyers, litigator Joe Groia and Justice Lori Douglas, in one case for so-called uncivil language in court and in the other for sexually explicit photos published on the Internet, raise questions about whether the reviews were worse than the conduct in question.

Two recent disciplinary proceedings against members of the legal profession make the people running things look a lot worse than the lawyers they are chasing.

The Law Society of Upper Canada (LSUC) has been persecuting Joe Groia since 2009. In June, an LSUC hearing panel found Groia guilty of professional misconduct, delivering an unconvincing 53-page pastiche of cut-and-paste reasons. And then there has been the bizarre spectacle of a Canadian Judicial Council (CJC) inquiry committee investigating the conduct of Lori Douglas, Associate Chief Justice of Manitoba.

I've written about Joe Groia before in these pages. Groia successfully defended John Felderhof of Bre-X Minerals notoriety on insider-trading charges. He was accused by judges of being strident and sarcastic in the proceedings, rude to the lawyer for the Ontario

Securities Commission, and prone to "rhetorical excess" and "petulant invective."

The LSUC hearing panel pontificated: "Lawyers have a duty to act in good faith, with respect and courtesy to the court, and to all persons with whom they deal in the course of their professional practice." It said, "a pattern of conduct that includes persistent attacks and sarcasm directed at opposing counsel can form the basis of incivility." The panel rejected the argument that a duty of civility can compromise a lawyer's duty to defend a client vigorously. It found Groia to be uncivil, a vague concept to say the least. Unless his appeal succeeds, Groia will be disciplined at a later hearing.

Joe Groia was certainly aggressive and blunt in the Felderhof litigation, even — God help us — sarcastic. This was particularly so when he was dealing with the lawyer for the Ontario Securities Commission (not a paragon of civility himself). But the LSUC hearing panel's bizarre condemnation of Groia as "uncivil" is reminiscent of Monty Python reporting that mythical London gangster Doug Piranha was feared because of his merciless use of "sarcasm, dramatic irony, metaphor, bathos, puns, parody, litotes and satire." What terrible things did Groia say? Well, for example, he used the word "Government" to refer to the Ontario Securities Commission. Goodness me.

Groia's representation of Felderhof may not have been advocacy's finest hour although, don't forget, his client was acquitted, job number one for a defence lawyer. His behaviour may have dragged out proceedings and made them unpleasant for all participants. For all I know, Joe Groia may not even be a very nice person (for the record, I've never met him). But for LSUC officials to spend so many resources and so much time over this matter makes them — in my opinion — look silly, even mysteriously vindictive. Aren't there more important issues facing the legal profession?

Most important of all, LSUC's pursuit of Groia is far more damaging to the judicial system than anything he is supposed to have done. As his counsel said in closing submissions to the hearing panel, "This prosecution… attacks the independence of the bar and freedom of expression, as counsel are now looking over their shoulders and censoring their vigorous representation of their clients, lest they face the type of ruinous prosecution the LSUC has visited on Mr. Groia."*

What about Lori Douglas, the Associate Chief Justice of Manitoba? If you haven't heard about the ongoing inquiry into her behaviour by the CJC, you must be deep in the wilderness, far from newspapers, free of the Internet. Lucky you.

The principal allegations against Justice Douglas are that in 2003 she and her lawyer husband sexually harassed of one of her husband's clients, including posting (by the husband) of graphic sexual photos on a web site, and that when she subsequently applied for a judicial appointment she answered "no" to the question "Is there anything in your past and present which could reflect negatively on yourself or the judiciary, and which should be disclosed?" A further allegation is that the continued availability of the photos on the Internet is "inherently contrary to the image and concept of integrity of the judiciary, such that the confidence of individuals appearing before the judge, or the public in its justice system, could be undermined."

Justice Douglas claims that when the alleged harassment took place she had no knowledge of her husband's "unimaginable betrayal" and "mad and undisclosed fantasy" and that any wrongdoing was entirely his. She denies concealing what had happened when she applied for a judicial appointment in 2005. (It is clear that the appointments committee knew about the Internet pictures, and the issue was flagged for consideration by Irwin Cotler, then minister of justice.) As for public confidence in the justice system, Douglas says "right thinking people do not conclude that a woman who has been victimized by her husband is to blame for her husband's conduct and, accordingly, lacks integrity or is not suitable to sit as a judge."

It is hard not to have sympathy for Justice Douglas. But it is damaging to the judiciary's *gravitas* to have this sad and sordid tale

---

*The fight between Groia and The Law Society of Upper Canada went on and on. In February 2017 the Supreme Court of Canada granted Groia leave to appeal a decision against him by the Ontario Court of Appeal. In the meantime, Groia was elected a Law Society bencher.

endlessly told and retold by the media. The inquiry itself has become a circus, with Douglas's lawyer filing an application with the Federal Court of Canada to quash the inquiry due to "a reasonable apprehension of bias" and the inquiry's "independent lawyer" claiming the inquiry has exceeded its jurisdiction and resigning. The CJC should have sought to settle the matter behind the scenes, transparency be damned. And it is difficult to imagine the Lori Douglas story eventually being put away and forgotten, with Justice Douglas quietly resuming her judicial duties. She should have recognized early on that the story itself, whatever her actual conduct, was "inherently contrary to the image and concept of integrity of the judiciary" and should have resigned. That would have restored some faith in her personal judgment.**

Two crazy proceedings, both damaging to the justice system. Save us from the disciplinarian.

**In November 2014, Judge Douglas agreed to early retirement if CJC proceedings were stayed. She retired in 2015.

POLITICS AND THE RULE OF LAW
JULY 2010

"Every Canadian lawyer should demand the return of Khadr to Canada." In January 2010 the Supreme Court of Canada ruled against the Canadian government for the second time in the long-running case of Omar Khadr, finding that his constitutional rights had been violated by brutal interrogation techniques while he was a prisoner at Guantanamo Bay. However, the government continued to refuse to seek his repatriation.

It's good to get back to basics occasionally. What is a lawyer's fundamental ethical obligation? Surely, the answer must be, to protect and promote the rule of law.

But, isn't the rule of law one of those vague concepts that means anything and everything to anybody? All of us, and the state itself, can surely commit to the idea without suffering any inconvenience.

Not so. Here is Tom Bingham's brilliant and measured new book, *The Rule of Law*. Bingham is a retired English judge, but not just any retired judge. He has been Master of the Rolls, Lord Chief Justice, and Senior Law Lord.* With elegance and forcefulness, Bingham describes what the rule of law means, and why it is more important today than ever.

---

*Lord Bingham died in September 2010.

Let me pick out three or four points he makes, from among many, that suggest some of the ethical responsibilities of the modern lawyer.

A recurring theme in Bingham's book is the limits imposed on the state by adherence to the rule of law. For example, torture is never acceptable, no matter what the circumstances. Bingham writes, "there are some practices so abhorrent as not to be tolerable, even when the safety of the state is said to be at risk, even where the price of restraint is that a guilty man may walk free. There are some things which even the supreme power in the state should not be allowed to do, ever."

A related point is the sweep of *habeas corpus*. Bingham picks the U.K. *Habeas Corpus Amendment Act* of 1679 as a milestone on the way to the rule of law. King Charles II's chief minister was in the habit of dispatching prisoners to distant parts of the United Kingdom where the writ of *habeas corpus* did not run. This meant that prisoners were unable to challenge the lawfulness of their detention, and that, of course, was the whole point. The 1679 *Amendment Act* stopped this abuse.

Now, we have the United States resorting to torture, something "the supreme power in the state should not be allowed to do, ever." Now, we have the United States, at Guantanamo Bay where a Canadian citizen — Omar Khadr — is detained, exactly emulating Charles II's approach to *habeas corpus* of more than three centuries ago. These are blatant breaches of the rule of law.

The fundamental ethical obligation of every lawyer is to resist this behaviour in any way legally possible. So, every Canadian lawyer should demand the return of Khadr to Canada. And, we should be very displeased that the Supreme Court of Canada recently refused to instruct the government to demand Khadr's repatriation, despite recognizing that his *Charter* rights had been breached.

But, isn't the post 9/11 world a new and terrifying place, one in which hoary concepts like the rule of law no longer apply the way they once did? Many, including high American officials, have argued that, in our new circumstances, discrimination against non-citizens (providing for their indefinite detention without charge, for example), or the erosion of fair hearing guarantees, or extraordinary rendition (which happened to Arar, with the connivance of our government), are justified. This is sometimes described as replacing a criminal justice model with a security model.

In reply, Bingham quotes the Council of Europe: "While the State has the right to employ to the full its arsenal of legal weapons to repress and prevent terrorist activities, it may not use indiscriminate measures which would only undermine the fundamental values they seek to protect. For a State to react in such a way would be to fall into the trap set by terrorism for democracy and the rule of law." Every lawyer should insist that no diminution of the rule of law ever take place.

A different kind of principle demanded by the rule of law is full access to justice. Bingham quotes the legal scholar E.J. Cohn: "Just as the modern State tries to protect the poorer classes against the common dangers of life, such as unemployment, disease, old age, social oppression, etc., so it should protect them when legal difficulties arise." And then Cohn adds an observation of great force: "…the case for such protection is stronger than the case for any other form of protection. The State is not responsible for the outbreaks of epidemics, for old age or economic crises. But the State is responsible for the law."

All members of the legal profession, as part of our commitment to the rule of law, should be concerned about the manifest inadequacies of the legal aid system, and work for a better way of promoting access to justice. Some time ago, in these pages, I urged a national legal insurance scheme. No one in the legal profession seemed interested. It wouldn't be easy to implement "judicare," and to do so would be controversial, just like establishment of the medicare system we now cherish, which was initially thought unworkable and was fought bitterly by many doctors. Absent something like judicare, well, as someone once said, "justice is open to all, like the Ritz Hotel."

Bingham's book has been described as part of the judicial trend towards idealistic constitutionalism incorporating a set of fundamental principles. Some find this worrying. As a reviewer in *The Times Literary Supplement* put it, as political conflict comes to be framed in legal terms, the political game has to find room for judges and lawyers. What of parliamentary sovereignty? Bingham is clear that, in the U.K. at least, legislation can only be struck down by judges if parliament itself has authorized such a process.

This, of course, is precisely what has happened in Canada with the *Charter of Rights and Freedoms*. The *Charter* put judges and lawyers right in the middle of the political game. With that, the fundamental ethical obligation of every Canadian lawyer, to promote and protect the rule of law, becomes even more important.

JURY SELECTION: RIGGING THE SYSTEM
JUNE 2009

"This is a big deal. It's an abuse of state power." In Barrie, Ontario, two lists of 120 potential jurors were ordered scrapped by a judge when secret background checks by the Crown on prospective jurors were revealed.

It turns out that Ontario police have been conducting background checks on prospective jurors. (Kudos to *The National Post* for breaking and pursuing this story.) Don't confuse this with traditional jury vetting, when both prosecution and defence publicly question, and perhaps challenge, prospective jurors in open court. What happened in Ontario was the secret gathering by police of information from confidential computer databases. This information was then handed over to Crown prosecutors, who apparently had asked for it in the first place. Prosecutors used this stuff to identify and pick jurors who might be more inclined to convict, and to weed out those who might be sympathetic to the accused. To add injury to insult, when the story came to light, the Crown tried to suppress it by seeking a publication ban. It's all reminiscent of the Stasi, East Germany's notorious secret police.

This is a big deal. It's an abuse of state power. It brings the administration of justice into question. Police and lawyers may have broken the law, and lawyers may be in breach of their own rules of professional conduct. Criminal defence lawyers, appalled by the whole thing, have started opening up old files to see if appeals are possible. Expect an avalanche of these appeals, at huge cost to the heavily burdened taxpayer. We should all be mighty angry about what has happened. What were the police and Crown attorneys thinking?

In Barrie, in June, two lists of 120 potential jurors were ordered scrapped by a judge when secret background checks on prospective jurors became known. Handwritten annotations next to some names on the lists noted *Highway Traffic Act* convictions, mental health problems, and the like. In some cases, the notes bordered on farce; "neighbour shot his cat" was one. Other names had "ok" written next to them. Did that mean they were likely to decide in the Crown's favour? One note next to a name was, "dislikes police."

But all right, it was only Barrie. An isolated incident, perhaps. But then, a few days later, a judge in Windsor declared a mistrial in a murder trial two months after it had begun because he discovered that police and Crowns had been up to the same thing. The Windsor police chief admitted that the practice was "routine." Almost immediately after that, it turned out that background checks on prospective jurors had also been conducted in Thunder Bay. Where else has it happened? No doubt we'll find out soon enough. There are 54 Crown offices in Ontario.

Ontario Attorney General Chris Bentley condemned the practice, claiming that it was not a "widespread issue" (how wide would it have to be before it could be considered "widespread"?). He ordered a provincial probe. Apparently a March 2006 directive from the Attorney General Michael Bryant had said only criminal record checks of prospective jurors could be conducted and all information must be shared with the defence; everyone seems to have forgotten about this. Ontario Provincial Police (OPP) Commissioner Julian Fantino has made a statement referring to "the practice of some of our OPP detachments of conducting background checks on potential jurors at the requests of local Crown Attorneys." Fantino ordered the practice stopped.

Ontario's privacy commissioner, Ann Cavoukian, began an investigation to see if privacy laws had been broken. A statement from her office said, "The focus of our investigation will be whether this was a proper use of police databases and whether the privacy rights of potential jurors have been compromised. … We will determine whether any provisions of Ontario's three privacy laws, the Freedom of Information and Protection of Privacy Act, the Municipal Freedom of Information and Protection of Privacy Act, and the Personal Health Information Protection Act, were breached." But Brian Beamish, assistant privacy commissioner, admitted that the privacy commissioner lacks subpoena powers on anything other than health-related information. She can order bodies to stop collecting information and destroy any information already collected, but can't compel them to participate or co-operate in an investigation.

Let's be clear about one thing. Background checks of potential jurors are illegal. Several sections of the Ontario *Juries Act* make plain that jury lists shall contain only the name, place of residence, and occupation of those on the list. And section 20 of the Act says, "The jury roll and every list containing the names of the jury drafted for any panel shall be kept under lock and key by the sheriff, and except in so far as may be necessary in order to prepare the panel lists, and serve the jury summons, shall not be disclosed …until ten days before the sittings of the court for which the panel has been drafted…" Chief Justice Beverley McLachlin, giving judgment for a unanimous Supreme Court of Canada, clearly and definitively described the jury selection process in the 2001 case of *R. v. Find*. She stressed the primacy of jury impartiality.

Perhaps Crown attorneys who were involved in all this should also worry about law society disciplinary action. Rule 4.06 (1) of Ontario's *Rules of Professional Conduct* says, "A lawyer shall encourage public respect for and try to improve the administration of justice." And commentary on rule 4.05(1) says, "a lawyer should not conduct or cause another, by financial support or otherwise, to conduct a vexatious or harassing investigation of either a member of the jury panel or a juror." It will be interesting to see if the law society steps up to the plate on this one. It may be a decisive test of the regulatory body

I'm not a great fan of judicial commissions of inquiry. So often, they are used by the powers that be to shunt problems aside and silence critics. But, in this case, we need one badly. The Ontario Ministry of the Attorney General is severely compromised. So are the police. The privacy commissioner is toothless. Only a judge can get to the bottom of this horrible mess.

ARE LAWYERS TO BLAME FOR THE MARKET COLLAPSE?

DECEMBER 2008

"What were the ethical responsibilities of these lawyers? Should they have said, this is a bad idea, no good can come of it, and I don't want to be involved?" When major investment banks failed and stocks went into freefall in September, 2008 there was an epidemic of finger pointing. The many highly paid lawyers who advised the firms that indulged in the orgy of borrowing that led to the collapse were seldom blamed.

Everyone's looking for someone to blame for the economic mess. It's satisfying to point the finger at American small-town mortgage lenders who gave money to people they must have known could never pay it back. And what about those investment bankers who packaged sub-prime mortgages into collateralized mortgage obligations (CMOs) that were fatally flawed? And the bond-rating agencies that gave triple-A ratings to junk? And those whiz kids who invented credit default swaps (CDSs) that magnified immeasurably the risks of something going wrong? Gosh darn it (as Sarah Palin might say), these people have a lot to answer for.

But wait a minute: What about the lawyers who were sitting at the table every step of the way? There were lawyers present when those sub-prime mortgages were handed out; when CMOs were structured; when bond-rating agencies did their work; and when CDSs were invented. Lawyers were particularly active at the upper end of the financial food chain. Clever and highly-paid attorneys on Wall Street (and Bay Street) had a big hand in inventing the fancy pieces of paper that have got us into so much trouble. (Full disclosure: In the early 1980s, I was one of several lawyers representing a New York investment bank that put together what I believe was the first mortgage-backed security issued in Canada.)

What were the ethical responsibilities of these lawyers? Should they have considered the broad economic consequences of their work? Should they have blown the whistle? Should they have said, this is a bad idea, no good can come of it, and I don't want to be involved?

Of course they shouldn't have. That, at least, is the traditional response. Lawyers, it goes, are not policemen, or self-appointed regulators, or priests. It's not the job of a lawyer to judge the economic impact, or the morality, of a transaction he's paid to facilitate. We all know, for example, that despicable criminals are entitled to vigorous legal representation. It's perfectly fine to help tax avoiders, even though aggressive tax avoidance harms the public fisc, leads to unacceptable disparities of wealth, and impedes great national policies that benefit the citizenry. And, so it goes, it's entirely ethical to lend a lawyerly hand with financial schemes, even though you suspect those schemes may imperil the economy and ruin millions of lives.

You can sum up the traditional view of legal professionalism this way: A lawyer is like a taxi driver. If a taxi driver picks up a passenger at the train station, and the passenger asks to go to the local whorehouse, the job of the taxi driver is to take him there safely. It's not his responsibility to try and convince the passenger that a trip to the art museum would be more edifying, and turn down the fare if he is unsuccessful in his exhortations.

I think this traditional view has had its day. For one thing, it has done a lot of damage to the standing of the legal profession. The public long ago noticed that many lawyers are not much more than amoral guns for hire, and is not appreciative of the fact. More than that, lawyers themselves seem increasingly discomfited about how they have drifted away from the social values embodied in the laws they work with. Moral neutrality and technical competence no longer seem enough, not even to most lawyers.

Do "cause lawyers" show the way? A cause lawyer is someone who commits himself and his legal skills to furthering a vision of the good society. This is all explained in *The Cultural Lives of Cause Lawyers*, a 2008 book edited by Austin Sarat and Stuart Scheingold, and published by Cambridge University Press. In the introduction, Sarat and Scheingold write, "by reconnecting lawyering with morality, cause lawyers make tangible the idea that lawyering is a 'public profession' and that its contribution to society goes beyond the aggregation, assembling, and deployment of technical skills." Cause lawyering, they write, "raises the political question of whose interests are served by the dominant understanding of legal professionalism."

I can hear the howls of protest. Does anyone seriously propose that a lawyer, before opening a file, should apply some kind of community-based moral test to see whether it's okay for him to take on the assignment? How on earth would that work? The suggestion seems even more preposterous if it implies, for example, that a securities lawyer should make some kind of complex economic judgment about the possible public effects of a proposed transaction. Quite apart from anything else, very few practising lawyers are competent to make such evaluations. Getting back to that economic mess, hardly an economist or financial expert saw it coming or, even today, fully understands what it's all about. What can you expect from a lawyer?

But these kinds of objections are only examples of the debating trick of *reductio ad absurdum* (Wikipedia: ".... a type of logical argument where one assumes a claim for the sake of argument and derives an absurd or ridiculous outcome, and then concludes that the original claim must have been wrong as it led to an absurd result.") They don't damage the proposition that a lawyer, as a well-educated creature of his community, should take into account the values and well being of that community when he does his work. Sometimes, notwithstanding the siren call of billable hours, he shouldn't open a file.

And so, if a lawyer, sitting in a conference room with his banker client, thinks that a mortgage applicant will soon default if given what he's asking for; or that a collateralized mortgage obligation is backed by loans that likely will collapse; or that a bond rating agency hasn't done its homework and is handing out ratings that will mislead investors; or that financial engineering is going on that could have incalculable adverse consequences; he should stand up, put his hat on, and walk out.

Let's see if the legal profession has learnt its lesson.

JUST DOING MY JOB

FEBRUARY 2009

"Moral neutrality, acceptable as it may be in general, doesn't mean that a lawyer should subvert the values of his society, or be blind to its best interests." Many lawyers who helped prepare the highly leveraged financial arrangements that led to the 2008-2009 recession claimed the protection of 'moral neutrality,' code for 'just doing my job.'

You never know when you'll hit a raw nerve.

My last ethics column argued that lawyers should take into account the values and well being of their community. I mentioned "cause lawyers," members of the legal profession who commit themselves to furthering a personal vision of a good society. The column didn't seem all that radical to me, but some readers took strong exception.

A tax practitioner (who, he said, had been practising tax law for 30 years) emailed that the cause lawyer concept "is just one more method that those who propagate politically correct action will use to constrain economic (read the market) activity to redesign society the way they see it." After explaining that tax evasion (that's right, tax evasion, not just avoidance) was a useful social activity, because an individual makes better use of the income he earns than any government, my tax practitioner correspondent concluded, "I suggest you get your facts right or perhaps you even acquaint yourself with the facts…"

Another email came from a senior and distinguished litigator, who seemed to be writing more in sorrow than in anger: "Perhaps one day you will write a column on the cause lawyer, often (or usually) single issue fanatics, who get so taken up with the cause that they have no shred of objectivity in advancing it, and thereby do a disservice to the cause, the courts, the profession and themselves." Ominously, he wrote, "I wonder if your view of lawyer morality would be the same if you needed to retain a lawyer."

Why are people riled up? Perhaps it's because they think my earlier article implied that there are only two kinds of lawyers, cause lawyers and guns for hire, and that the first is morally superior to the second. It might follow, I suppose, that a member of the legal profession should sign on to cause lawyering if he wants to be good person. That's too much for anyone to swallow. Let me quote from T.S. Eliot's poem *The Love Song of J. Alfred Prufrock*: "That is not what I meant, at all."

I don't think anyone wants to deliver the legal profession to single issue fanatics. (Although, let's not forget that some of those single issue fanatics have latched onto a pretty important single issue to be fanatical about — the wrongfully convicted, for example.) But surely you can reject the extremes of cause lawyering without rushing helter-skelter to the other end of the spectrum, into the full and seductive embrace of the gun for hire alternative. Where might one reasonably stop along the way?

Many lawyers find moral neutrality — "objectivity," if you want to call it that — the most appropriate stance. The job of a lawyer, they say, is simply to represent the client; what the lawyer thinks of the client and his case, from the point of view of morality or community values, is irrelevant. Everyone, no matter how abhorrent, is entitled to legal representation.

When Ramsey Clark, U.S. attorney-general under President Lyndon Johnson, joined Saddam Hussein's defence team, he was savagely attacked. His response? "That Hussein and other former Iraqi officials must have lawyers of their choice to assist them in defending against the criminal charges brought against them ought to be self-evident among a people committed to truth, justice and the rule of law. …[A lawyer] should accept such service as his highest duty." Ironically, many cause lawyers would recognize and endorse this sentiment. It is, after all, a personal commitment to a cause.

But moral neutrality, acceptable as it may be in general, doesn't mean that a lawyer should subvert the values of his society, or be blind to its best interests. Canadian law societies make this plain in their rules. The Canons of Ethics of the Law Society of British Columbia, for example, says that "it is a lawyer's duty to promote the interests of the state," and that "a lawyer owes a duty to the state, to maintain its integrity and its law." (Note, not just its law — its integrity as well.) The rules of professional conduct in Ontario say that, when acting as an advocate, the lawyer shall not "knowingly assist or permit the client to do anything that the lawyer considers to be dishonest or dishonourable."

In a paper entitled "A Lawyer's Duty to Society," delivered to a 2008 Ontario Advocates Society symposium on professionalism, Sylvia Corthorn and Reena Goyal drew a distinction between the "thin" and "thick" views of professionalism. People who believe in the "thin" view argue "that there is no residual duty to society if the lawyer's duties to the client, the courts and the Law are discharged." The "thick" view, on the other hand, requires that the lawyer's duty to society be paramount; "To act in a way that might reasonably be foreseen to be contrary to the public interest is inconsistent with the defining characteristic of a profession." The Corthorn/Goyal paper implies that law society rules favour the thick view. This may come as a surprise to lawyers who like to argue in favour of moral neutrality and consider themselves to be in the main stream.

As for me, I'm sticking to my guns. I think it's very hard, for example, for a lawyer to justify, on the grounds of moral neutrality, having been a cog in the machine that packaged and sold collateralized debt obligations (CDOs) made up of sub-prime mortgages unlikely ever to be paid. These CDOs were irresponsibly graded by rating agencies enmeshed in conflicts of interest, and were then off-loaded onto unsuspecting buyers who didn't really understand what they're getting. Ignorance is the usual defence in this and similar cases (who knew?), but what about due diligence, a concept much loved by the legal profession (at least, when it comes to other people)?

And as for it being okay for a lawyer to help a client evade taxes — puhleese!

LEGAL PRACTICE AND SOCIAL CHANGE

BOUNDARIES
AUGUST 2016

"For most lawyers, the demands and problems and attitudes of legal practice are with them always, seeping into every pore of their being." Lawyers are steeped in the traditional principles of the adversarial system, which sometimes seem to apply to everything. Where are the boundaries, professional and personal?

A friend of mine runs a children's rights centre in San Francisco. The centre has a professional staff of about thirty. It's a mix of lawyers and social workers. I asked my friend what differences she found between the two professions. Boundaries, she said. Social workers understand boundaries. Lawyers don't get it. Social workers are taught about boundaries right from the beginning. No one ever talks about boundaries in law school. It's a problem for lawyers, my friend told me. In her view, not having a clear sense of boundaries makes lawyers less effective in their work.

I think there are two kinds of boundaries, active and passive. Active boundaries govern the interaction between professionals and their clients and are driven by the fiduciary nature of the relationship. They are easily expressed as rules or guidelines. For a long time the medical profession has been particularly sensitive to active boundaries in a therapeutic setting. There is a substantial literature on the subject. The list of exhortations to doctors and nurses seems endless. No sharing of personal information. No nicknames or endearments.

No romantic or sexual involvement. The list goes on and on. Active boundaries have been similarly explored in the teaching profession. Don't be Facebook friends with a student. Don't send a student a personal email. Don't drive him home after class. No touching. Etc. etc.

Then there are passive boundaries. These are subtler and cannot easily be expressed in rules. They are the boundaries that allow professionals to prevent their work-related concerns intruding on and damaging their personal life. Don't bring your clients' problems home with you. Don't treat your loved ones as if they were patients or clients or pupils. Have an autonomous life. Distance, distance, distance. Who could survive as a pediatric oncologist without well-developed passive boundaries, without leaving the illness and death of children at the hospital door, heartless as that sounds?

So what about lawyers? The profession hasn't really dealt with active boundaries. There are a few warnings scattered about, here and there, not many. The Washington State Bar Association, for example, warns its members of signs that they may be at risk of violating boundaries. These signs include altering the established management of communication (either more or less than the customary frequency of phone calls, written correspondence, emails and texts); changing billing practices (special financial arrangements, allowing bills to go unpaid); and providing special treatment (meeting at odd hours, providing your home phone number, allowing "drop in" appointments, agreeing to unusual requests).

Why should we care about the violation of active boundaries, about signs like those identified by the Washington State Bar Association? The argument is that once objectivity is lost — once the client becomes more than just a client — two bad things happen. First, the quality of legal advice and practice declines. Second, the fiduciary relationship — created by the imbalance of power and knowledge, characterized by trust and confidence — is violated. As the fiduciary relationship collapses, conflict of interest arises and the client may be exploited.

Is this argument sound? I'm not sure it is. Why should the quality of advice decline if a client becomes a friend? You can cogently argue that the opposite might happen. As for exploitation of the client, that depends. Take romantic relationships. If it's between a family law practitioner and a distraught, penniless, abused wife seeking a divorce, well, a "romantic" relationship is a bad idea. It's not as clear if the female senior partner of a big firm strikes up a relationship with the chief executive of a hedge fund that is a client. As they say, ethics are often situational. Circumstances matter.

My San Francisco friend mostly had passive boundaries in mind when she compared social workers and lawyers. Social workers seem to be able to circumscribe their work life with some success, but for most lawyers the demands and problems and attitudes of legal practice are with them always, seeping into every pore of their being. Lawyers are propelled by ambition, driven by the double tyranny of billable hours and an adversarial system, caught up in the pervasive business model view of legal practice, oppressed by the demands of digital devices. The consequences can be dire — neurosis, depression, substance abuse, breakdown in personal relations. The incidence of suicide among lawyers is one of the highest among the professions. An oft-cited 1991 Johns Hopkins University study reported that lawyers suffer from major depressive disorder at a rate 3.6 times higher than non-lawyers who share their key socio-demographic traits.

Draft rules, suggested guidelines, hortatory statements by leaders of the bar, speeches by associate professors, continuing education conferences, opinion pieces like this one — none of these can address this problem in any way that matters. That's because the problem comes from a deep-seated culture, almost impossible to change, that has the legal profession in its tenacious grip. The essence of this culture is that being a lawyer is no longer any different from any other occupation — investment banker, say, or a buyer of old gold, or a real estate agent. Legal practice is not in the deepest sense a "profession," an occupation with an explicit commitment to the public good (that commitment, of course, does not preclude making a living). In the case of lawyers, the public good is a functioning and accessible legal system that provides justice for all. We lawyers have conspicuously failed to create and sustain such a system. We live in a country where the vast majority cannot afford legal services and are therefore denied access to justice. Sometimes we pretend otherwise, but that is a *lebenslüge*, a delusion that allows us to live.

The definition of what a lawyer is and does is blurred, indistinct, vague. What sets legal practice apart is no longer clear. That makes the acknowledgement of coherent boundaries, active and particularly passive, difficult, perhaps impossible. Clients may suffer as a consequence. But we lawyers suffer more than anyone.

SEX CRIMES: WHO'S ON TRIAL?

DECEMBER 2015

"In one crucial aspect, sexual assault trials are very much like any other criminal trial. The accused has the fearsome power of the state arrayed against him." There is an increasingly passionate but also chaotic debate over appropriate tactics and strategy when it comes to defending clients accused of sex crimes. What is the appropriate balance between a fair trial and 'whacking the complainant?'

What are the ethical boundaries for a lawyer defending someone accused of a sex crime? Is he a hired gun, expected to do everything legally possible to win the case, concerned only about the fate of his client, free to attack the complainant unreservedly in cross-examination, dedicated — as it is sometime put — to proof, not truth? That, I think, was the old idea, unchallenged for many years.

Or does the defence lawyer have broader social obligations that mitigate his responsibility to the accused, obligations that include not embracing myths and stereotypes about women and sex and giving special consideration to the complainant? That is more modern thinking, lets call it the "New View," born of high minded concern for the well being and rights of those alleging sexual assault, and promoted by a new generation of academics and ethicists.

David Tanovich, of Windsor's Faculty of Law, succinctly expresses the New View in a series of rhetorical questions: "The fundamental questions all defence counsel should ask in sexual assault cases include whether their conduct ... is grounded in stereotypes about sexual assault and gender, sexual orientation, race or disability? Will their tactics in cases of truthful complainants cause irreparable harm? Will it perpetuate disadvantage such as dissuading other complainants from seeking justice in the criminal justice system? Will it bring the administration of justice into disrepute?" Professor Tanovich believes that any conduct by a defence lawyer that promotes or exploits stereotypes violates his ethical duty not to act in a discriminatory fashion. "This would include cross-examination on what the complainant was wearing, whether she immediately reported the incident, whether she spoke to a psychiatrist, her socio-economic status, drug or alcohol use, lifestyle, or marital status."

Tanovich's ideas are representative of the views of most members of the contemporary professoriat who bother with the issue. But what do so-called sexual assault lawyers, the people on the front lines, think? Professor Elaine Craig of Dalhousie Law School has looked into the matter. She conducted 20 "semi-structured interviews" with experienced criminal lawyers in four Canadian provinces (British Columbia, Ontario, Nova Scotia and Newfoundland). Her findings appear in a paper entitled "The Ethical Identity of Sexual Assault Lawyers." What Professor Craig discovered was a state of bewilderment. Canadian sexual assault lawyers don't seem to know what to think about the relationship between professional obligations and ethical duties.

Craig writes: "Members of the criminal defence bar have been rightly criticized for perpetuating a 'whack the complainant strategy' that discourages victims of sexual violence from coming forward, and traumatizes those that do report sexual offences." But she finds, based admittedly on a small sample, that not all defence lawyers feel this way. None of her interviewees explicitly invoked the hired gun metaphor. Their thinking was often incoherent. Writes Craig, "Most of the interview participants offered comments that seemed at odds with other responses they had provided." She concludes that — in Canada at least — there is more than one professional vision of how to practice sexual assault law. Sexual assault lawyers, it seems, are torn between Scylla and Charybdis, finding it difficult to choose between unfettered loyalty to their client and vague obligations to the complainant, society, and the justice system.

Craig and Tanovich often refer in their writings to the "context" of sexual assault cases. By this they imply that sexual assault cases exist in a separate world where unique ethical considerations apply. There is no question that sexual assault cases, by their very nature, are unpleasant if not awful for those involved, and arguably this may impose particular obligations, if only those of human decency, on all those caught up in the process. But this is true, in different ways, of many criminal trials (and, indeed, of trials in general). Human happiness does not flourish in the courtrooms of the nation. No one enjoys being cross-examined. It is hard to see that sexual assault trials are *sui generis*, completely unlike any other, requiring special ethical rules.

Indeed, in one crucial respect sexual assault trials are very much like any other criminal trial. The accused, yet to be found guilty, perhaps eventually to be found innocent, has the fearsome power of the state arrayed against him. He stands to lose his liberty, let alone his reputation, livelihood, and God knows what else. His fate depends in part on our system of law and justice, and the unceasing and energetic efforts, and skill and loyalty, of his advocate. In our system, in our country, he is entitled to these things. Were the process to be excessively complainant centric, the accused's access to loyal and zealous advocacy might be in doubt and his reliance on justice misplaced.

To return to Professor Craig's findings, it is small wonder that Canadian criminal defence lawyers are confused when it comes to sexual assault cases. The New View, and perceived political correctness frequently and vociferously expressed, pushes them in one direction. Their natural instincts and a long tradition push them in another. What are they to do? Almost no one denies the sensitivity of the issues and the need for balance and maturity. To arrive at the right balance is hard indeed. Pity the poor lawyer.

One more thing. These days someone who alleges sexual assault is often carelessly described as a "victim." This is not right. The dictionary definition of "victim" is "a person harmed… as a result of a crime…" The use of the word "victim" assumes that a crime has been committed and that the accused is guilty. Let us remember, the whole point of a fair trial is to determine if that is the case.

THE DIGITAL MOB
AUGUST 2015

"Until recently, it seemed that the lynch mob was extinct, but sadly like a monster in a horror movie, it has been born again, this time wearing a digital disguise." When former Canadian Broadcasting Corporation radio host Jian Ghomeshi was charged with sexual assault, the outpouring of digital invective against him was overwhelming.

Billie Holiday, in her 1939 song "Strange Fruit," sang: "Black bodies swinging in the southern breeze, Strange fruit hanging from the poplar trees." She was singing about lynch mobs. In the southern United States, in the late 19th century and first half of the 20th century, mobs of white people lynched black men for crimes that were presumed and never proven. Historians estimate that about 3,500 black men were murdered in this way. With some notable exceptions, the legal profession looked the other way.

The lynch mob was a repudiation of everything that is good about the law.

Until recently, it seemed extinct, a relic of a horrible bygone age, but sadly, like a monster in a horror movie, it has been born again, this time wearing a digital disguise. Twitter, Facebook, and their pale imitators, allow, even encourage, the instant assembly of a group whose members come together to self-righteously condemn and destroy someone who, for whatever reason, has offended them.

Members of such a vigilante group typically are vague on the facts and have not thought seriously about the issues. They are nothing more than a mob baying for blood.

This appalling development is sometimes called "public shaming." Probably the most famous victim of digital public shaming is Justine Sacco, whose 2014 Tweet from Heathrow Airport before she boarded a flight to Cape Town, an inept attempt at irony and humour, was interpreted as racist by some ("Going to Africa. Hope I don't get AIDS. Just kidding. I'm white!"). By the time Sacco's flight landed, through a process of re-Tweeting coupled with extreme (and sometimes obscene) comments, she was infamous, her reputation was in tatters, and she had been fired by her employer. Sacco has yet to reconstruct her life.

Which brings me to Jian Ghomeshi. You may remember (I bet you do) that in October 2014 allegations surfaced from a variety of sources that Ghomeshi had sexually assaulted several women. The so-called Twittersphere exploded. Initially there were expressions of support for Ghomeshi and doubt about the allegations, but the tide quickly turned. After the first few hours, almost all those who tweeted about Ghomeshi assumed the allegations were true and reviled him in extravagant terms. Within a few days, he was fired from his talk show job. His public relations firm dumped him. His friends turned their backs. His publisher cancelled a book contract. His agent dropped him. He went to California to hide out. All this took place *before* criminal charges were laid — that happened about a month later. Whatever the outcome of his trial — and he may be found not guilty* — his life and career have been substantially damaged if not completely wrecked.

Then there is the recent case of Minnesota dentist Dr. Walter Palmer, by now the most famous dentist in the world. Earlier this year, he used a bow and arrow to shoot Cecil the Lion in Zimbabwe, apparently contrary to local law. At the end of July, news and photos about Dr. Palmer killing Cecil somehow got onto Twitter, and Dr.

---

*In March 2016, in the first of two scheduled trials, Ghomeshi was found not guilty of all charges. He avoided the second trial, on additional charges, by signing a peace bond.

Palmer's world went mad. On just one day, July 29, there were close to a million Tweets about the incident, almost all of them hideously critical of Palmer and many calling for his blood in the most vivid terms. As several journalists put it, "The hunter became the hunted." Palmer's home was vandalized. He was expelled from his dentistry practice. He went into hiding. He feared for his life. Ghomeshi and Palmer are by no means isolated examples of the crude persecution that social media makes possible.

Anyone can be unjustly accused of anything. For starters, you can be accused of not being a nice person (e.g., "Hey buddy, you're a racist!") There are laws and codes of behaviour that offer some protection against this kind of accusation, although they're largely ineffectual, as anyone knows who has been the object of unfounded rumour or gossip. Much more seriously, like Jian Ghomeshi and Walter Palmer, you can be accused of criminal behaviour. There are traditional systems and rules to ensure, so far as possible, that, in the case of crimes, guilt is clearly established before punishment is imposed. There's that thing called "presumption of innocence." But the Ghomeshi and Palmer cases dramatically illustrate that these systems and rules don't apply to a social media mob, which will pronounce you guilty and impose punishment in the twinkle of an eye. In this way, social media subverts and undermines a critical part of the criminal justice system that many people, particularly lawyers, laboured mightily for many years to put in place.

How do you mesh the demands of the traditional criminal justice system, developed carefully over centuries, with the reality of the new world of social media, a chaotic behemoth barely a decade old? Part of the tension is between the right to free expression and other individual rights that can be threatened by freedom of expression. How to resolve that tension is an enduring and delicate political and ethical conundrum. Most would agree on one thing: free expression does not trump everything. But when should it give way?

The legal profession has an ethical obligation to protect the criminal justice system by pushing back vigorously against untrammeled public shaming, particularly when it involves accusations of criminal behaviour. But how? For one thing, by going public when necessary. So, for example, in the case of Jian Ghomeshi, leaders of the profession and bar associations should have entered the social media debate and publicly cautioned about presuming guilt. They should have used the very same tools used by the lynch mob. They should have played on the same playing field. They should have tweeted their hearts out.

In the new world, the old, ponderous and slow ways of expressing an opinion are no longer good enough for anyone, including members of the legal profession.

THE DEPRESSED LAWYER
AUGUST 2014

"The deadliest source of demoralization is the degeneration of law from a profession into a business." Lawyers are supposed to be hard-nosed, ambitious, unafraid of conflict, and competitive. But many lawyers are depressed, often severely, and the changing nature of legal practice may be to blame.

William Styron in *Darkness Visible*, his extraordinary memoir, wrote, "The pain of severe depression is quite unimaginable to those who have not suffered it…" The sufferer, wrote Styron, "must, despite the anguish devouring his brain, present a face approximating the one that is associated with ordinary events and companionship. He must try to utter small talk, and be responsive to questions, and knowingly nod and frown and, God help him, even smile."

Lawyers suffer from what some call "the terrible melancholy" more than any other professional group. A frequently cited 1991 Johns Hopkins study found that lawyers suffer from major depressive disorder at a rate 3.6 times higher than non-lawyers who share their socio-demographic traits. The search "lawyers + depression" produces 13 million hits on Google. There is even a web site called "lawyerswithdepression." The well-publicized suicide this past summer of Cheryl Hanna, a prominent law professor at the University of Vermont, reminded us of this awful problem. Hanna, who had been hospitalized for depression, left her psychiatric hospital, bought a gun, and shot herself. She was 48 years old.

Why write about lawyers and depression in a column about ethics? Depression is a disease, you might say; it's a serious illness, not a moral quandary. But depression dulls the moral senses. It impedes rational and responsible decision-making. The depressed person may no longer be able to make sound ethical judgments, or may simply not care about ethical issues. He may indeed, when speaking with clients, "utter small talk, and be responsive to questions, and knowingly nod and frown," but his psychology is undermined and his judgment impaired. And depressed people often self-medicate with alcohol or drugs which, of course, just makes everything a lot worse. Depression in lawyers may be the legal profession's biggest underlying ethical issue.

Explanations for depression in lawyers abound. They often start by considering the kind of people attracted to the legal profession. Chances are those who aspire to become lawyers like conflict and look forward to putting some stick about (fans of Francis Urquhart will know what that means). They're ambitious and competitive, rather than accepting and contemplative. They're smart instead of intellectual. They like money, and hunger for prestige. These predispositions do not favour happiness.

Once embarked on his profession, the legal tyro finds himself in a perilous environment. Martin Seligman, a psychologist and former president of the American Psychological Association, has identified several characteristics of legal practice that demoralize practitioners. First, there is the prevalence of pessimism. Seligman writes, "Pessimism is seen as a plus among lawyers, because seeing troubles as pervasive and permanent is a component of what the law profession deems prudence." But the personal consequences of pessimism can be devastating: "Lawyers who can see clearly how badly things might turn out for their clients can also see clearly how badly things might turn out for themselves." Another psychological factor demoralizing lawyers is what Seligman calls "low decision latitude in high-stress situations." This is a particular problem for junior lawyers who often work long hours under stringent deadlines, and yet have very little control over what they do and how they do it.

But the deadliest source of demoralization is the degeneration of law from a profession into a business. Seligman writes that law has "migrated from being a practice in which good counsel about justice and fairness was the primary good to being a big business in which billable hours, take-no-prisoners victories, and the bottom line are now the principle ends." This occurs in the context of the adversary system, which promotes a "win/loss" mentality. A win/loss mentality, in a business setting without old-fashioned professional ideals to mitigate it, leads to anger, anxiety and sadness.

Compounding the problem is the stigma that attaches to mental illness, a stigma that promotes secrecy and shame. Psychiatrist David Goldbloom, chair of the Mental Health Commission of Canada, has said, "If you're run over by a bus, your colleagues are very sympathetic. But if you throw yourself in front of a bus... " Michael Redhill, a distinguished writer who has suffered from depression for 40 years, wrote in a recent essay, "I am ashamed to admit that I am a sufferer."

A lawyer who is depressed will feel the stigma and the shame more than most. He will find it difficult to admit his illness and seek help. He will be afraid to do so. Depression throws cognitive capacity, the very essence of a lawyer's standing and identity, into doubt. Admitting depression undermines a legal practice, as skeptical clients look elsewhere and cautious colleagues consult somebody else.

I'm astonished that the law societies of Canada seem to have little or no interest in this fundamental problem. The issue of depression generally only surfaces in disciplinary proceedings, when a lawyer in trouble offers his state of mind as an explanation for professional misfeasance. A handful of official counseling services for lawyers do exist, but they are not well known. The depressed lawyer, struggling mightily, frightened to recognize or admit his problem, is offered no help or guidance and has nowhere to turn. Law societies prefer to impose discipline than provide assistance.

The legal profession must do three things to confront this profound problem. First, members of the profession must talk widely and honestly about depression and its causes. Second, to the extent possible, we must remove the stigma of depression, and emotionally acknowledge what we intellectually know, that it is an illness and not a defect of character. Third, suitable medical help must be made easily available for those who need it.

Things can get better. In his essay discussing his own depression, Michael Redhill writes, "The depressed person wants to live and wants to love." He quotes the final line of Dante's *Inferno*: "Thence we came forth to rebehold the stars."

WHEN MONEY IS ALL THAT MATTERS
JUNE 2014

"It's extraordinary what a clever lawyer will endure, the opportunities he will forgo, for marginal increases in an already substantial income." The rates that lawyers charge their clients continue to climb, leaving behind more and more of those needing legal services, yet lawyers, although richer, seem no happier. Why?

Adam Liptak is the Supreme Court correspondent of *The New York Times* (NYT). He also writes "Sidebar," a frequent *NYT* column about developments in the law. Liptak is a graduate of Yale Law School. He worked in a Wall Street law firm for four years, and then moved to *The Times* legal department before becoming a legal journalist. He's a smart man.

On May 17, Liptak was given an honourary doctorate by Florida's Stetson University. He gave the commencement address. Liptak told the new graduates, "Don't make it all about the money." He riffed on this theme. "Don't get used to the money," he said. "Life is not a purely economic matter.... Make a difference rather than a buck."

Liptak points out that if you make it all about the money, you won't be able to accept your dream job when it's offered. You won't be able to follow your heart. Dream jobs, in government or public service or journalism or education, generally come with pay cuts. He urges: "Don't find yourself in this position: You are terribly unhappy in your work (and a lot of lawyers are.) You want to make a change.

But you are locked into a mortgage and lifestyle that will not allow you to do something else, something that brings you satisfaction, if not joy, and something that makes the world a better place."

Liptak has walked the walk. When he went from Wall Street to *The Times* legal department, he took a pay cut. When he went from the legal department to being a reporter, he took another pay cut. But being a reporter for *The New York Times* was his dream job. He followed his heart. "As a purely economic matter, I suppose I made stupid choices," he says. "But life is not purely an economic matter."

Liptak was happy to leave Wall Street, although he admits he learned a ton there and was surrounded by very smart people. He is not an admirer of big firm culture. Law firms, he argues, are built on two crippling ethical tensions. One is hourly billing: "It leads to punishing work schedules, unhappy lawyers, ill-served clients, over-lawyered cases, perverse incentives, and outright fraud." The other ethical tension is created by the adversarial system: better lawyers get better results, and this can easily lead to injustice.

When he was on Wall Street, Liptak says, "We spared no expense. We scorched the earth. It was exciting." Anyone who has worked in a big firm knows what he is talking about, the frisson of the big deal, of the hostile takeover, of headline-grabbing litigation. But his experience on Wall Street, says Liptak, his immersion in the adversarial system, "coarsened my behaviour." It led him to make what he calls "jerk moves."

I called Liptak at the Washington bureau of *The New York Times* to talk to him about his Stetson speech. He expanded on the corrosive effect of money. "On Wall Street everyone cares too much about how much the other guy is making. Most of the big law firms report profit-per-partner to *American Lawyer* magazine, which publishes a ranking. You know how much the guy across the street is making. And it's deeply upsetting if he's making more than you."

I asked him, why is money so important to lawyers? "If you don't find your work satisfying," said Liptak, "and don't think it's valuable, well, then, what's left? All that's left is money, and so money is all that matters."

As for jerk moves, Liptak told me, "One of the problems of legal practice on Wall Street, maybe just about everywhere, is it's valuable to be seen as *tough*. Why is that? There's a reason it's called the 'justice system,' and not the 'legal system.' The point of law is justice. How does being *tough* promote justice? How does being a jerk do anybody any good?" (An additional problem: if you're a big jerk at the office, you're probably a big jerk at home as well. It's hard to compartmentalize.)

These admonitions and criticisms are not new. Warnings about the danger of pursuing money to the exclusion of everything else can be found in the Bible. Almost all observers of the legal profession agree that hourly billing is a terrible system (I've been attacking it for years.) Most lawyers don't want to be a jerk, stupidly throwing their weight around at the office and at home (there are exceptions — I once had a partner who liked to say that to be a good lawyer you had to be prepared to bite the legs off metal chairs — a puzzling metaphor). When it comes to the merits of the adversary system, opinion is divided, although Liptak's point that the best lawyers usually win, and this warps the justice system, cannot be gainsaid: only corporations, government and wealthy individuals can afford the best lawyers, and that gives them a huge advantage. Don't be poor if you want justice.

As for hourly billing, a stupider system of assigning value to professional services has never been invented. It's harmful to lawyers and clients alike. Everyone knows it. Yet, it will not go away, for reasons I cannot understand.

What is puzzling is the great strength of these bad attitudes, foolish ideas and structural flaws in law and the legal profession. In particular, it's extraordinary what a clever lawyer will endure, the opportunities he will forego, for marginal increases in an already substantial income. Is it failure of the imagination, existential fear of the abyss, or just an irrational overwhelming desire for a bigger house and fancier car? I don't know.

Perhaps Gordon Gekko was right in the movie *Wall Street*: "Greed, for lack of a better word, is good. Greed is right. Greed works."

THE NAKED JUDGE
DECEMBER 2013

"The Lori Douglas affair makes the judiciary look bad to the man on the street, and that's a big deal." In November 2013 the members of a committee reviewing the appointment of Justice Lori Douglas, whose former husband posted nude pictures of her on the Internet, resigned en masse.

Is there no end to the Lori Douglas circus, an apparently interminable saga of personal and institutional misjudgment?

In case you've spent the last few years in a cabin in the woods cut off from what passes as civilization, or on Mars, let me explain in brief what's been going on. Lori Douglas is the Associate Chief Justice of Manitoba. Before she was appointed to the bench in 2005, salacious nude photos of Justice Douglas were posted on the Internet by her husband, Jack King, apparently without her knowledge, although she later discovered what he had done. It is alleged that King, a practising lawyer, also tried to arrange for Douglas to have sex with one of his clients who then claimed he had been sexually harassed.

To cut a long and depressing story short, the Lori Douglas affair ended up before the Canadian Judicial Council (CJC), the national body charged with disciplining judges. That is when it went from being a titillating narrative of questionable individual conduct to an alarming example of judicial dysfunction. This past November, after more than two years of messing about, members of the CJC inquiry committee considering the complaint against Douglas resigned *en masse*, giving angry written reasons for why they were quitting. Back to square one.

The doomed inquiry committee was appointed in September 2011. It wasn't long before Douglas's counsel, Sheila Block, went to the Federal Court of Canada alleging that the committee was biased and seeking judicial review of its proceedings. The law seemed to require that the commission be represented by the Attorney General of Canada, but the Attorney General had a problem. How could he get involved at this early stage when, as Minister of Justice, he would eventually have to deal impartially with the committee's recommendation, perhaps asking Parliament to remove a sitting judge? Eventually, the Attorney General announced that he intended to "remain neutral" and take no position on the merits of Lori Douglas's judicial review application. Justice Douglas and her various allegations were therefore, in effect, unopposed in Federal Court, and she obtained a stay of the inquiry committee's proceedings.

In its resignation reasons, the committee castigated the Attorney General. "The AGC's decision to remain neutral means that the judicial conduct process and an inquiry committee's role in it will never be able to be defended since this same conflict will arise every time a judge brings a judicial review application against an inquiry committee. …If the process is allowed to be sidetracked in this way, a knowledgeable public would think that a judicial conduct process has been created which is, by its nature, doomed to delay, wasted costs, confusion, inconsistency and perhaps, in the end, failure. And it would be hard to disagree with them."

The committee members quit in a snit. They thought it was better for everybody — particularly them — if they left. If there were to be a new inquiry committee, they said, it would be pointless for Lori Douglas to go ahead with judicial review of the prior committee's proceedings. "It is ironic that the only way this Committee can meet the transparency requirements so essential for public confidence and inform the public of this critical flaw in the process is to resign but, regrettably, that appears to be the case."

The public is entitled to be outraged by this shambles. No one comes out of it looking good. Who should we be mad at, and why?

Justice Douglas, for starters. As I wrote in this column over a year ago, it is hard not to have some sympathy for her predicament, but it's clear she's too compromised to sit as a judge again. She should have realized early on that her position was untenable and the good of the justice system required her resignation. It was her duty to resign. That, and perhaps only that, would have restored some faith in Justice Douglas' judgment and integrity.

Then there's the CJC inquiry committee, chaired by Chief Justice Catherine Fraser of Alberta. The general view in the legal profession is that the committee made a hash of things, losing control of its proceedings and leaving itself open to charges of bias. Sheila Block certainly thought the committee was biased, and it seems she was not alone. In August 2012 the committee's independent counsel, Guy Pratte, a senior and respected lawyer, resigned. Word has it that Pratte thought the committee was interfering with his independent status and taking an inappropriately aggressive attitude towards witnesses. Pratte's lengthy resignation letter so far has not been made public.

And then there's the law itself. The committee, inept as it seems to have been, had a point when it comes to judicial review of its proceedings by the Federal Court. It's not even clear that the Federal Court has jurisdiction over the committee, which is not an administrative tribunal, but has the status of a superior court given it by the *Judges Act*. If the committee is subject to the Federal Court's jurisdiction, then it should have proper legal representation by counsel it retains (as distinct from the independent counsel which it appoints). Otherwise, as the committee noted, the likely outcome is "delay, wasted costs, confusion, inconsistency and perhaps, in the end, failure." Time for the law to be clarified or changed.

All this may seem like inside baseball, too esoteric to matter much to the general public. Not so. The Lori Douglas affair makes the judiciary look bad to the man on the street, and that's a big deal. An individual judge who should depart is clinging on for dear life (and a fat pay check). The *risqué* facts have attracted widespread media attention. There doesn't seem to be any quick and fair way of considering whether a judge should be disciplined. The law looks like an ass.

There are no heroes in this tawdry tale.*

---

*As noted earlier, in November 2014 Judge Douglas agreed to early retirement if CJC proceedings were stayed. She retired in 2015.

EVIL CLIENTS
AUGUST 2013

"The world legal profession yawned and looked the other way."
In July 2013 a U.K.-based group issued guidelines for lawyers who
encounter human rights violations by their clients in overseas
locations. The guidelines were issued in the context of recently
issued United Nations principles on the same topic.

What do you do if a corporate client doing business overseas disdains local human rights? It would be easy to flounder around, rudderless.

The United Nations to the rescue! In 2011, the U.N. Human Rights Council unanimously approved "The Guiding Principles on Business and Human Rights," generally known as the UNGP. The UNGP's basic principles are "protect, respect and remedy." The state has a duty to protect human rights. The private sector has a responsibility to respect them. Both states and the private sector must provide remedies for abuses. Here's the interesting part: in the UNGP, these principles apply at home *and abroad*.

The world legal profession yawned and looked the other way. In 2012, the American Bar Association (ABA) House of Delegates endorsed the UNGP, but, as far as one can tell, ABA approval has had no effect on how U.S. law firms behave. In Canada, the Guiding Principles have attracted a smidgen of academic attention, but no interest from the practising bar. The Canadian Bar Association (CBA) has been silent on the subject. International human rights? Who cares?

But an interesting thing happened in Britain this past July. The London-based A4ID ("Advocates for International Development") issued a guide to the UNGP for the legal profession. *American Law Litigation Daily* described it as a "primer on how to handle your evil clients." The guide's general idea is that lawyers should use their "leverage" with clients to get them to avoid or stop human rights violations, and must not themselves contribute to such violations.

The A4ID document is poorly written and sadly hortatory, although it is enlivened a little by hypotheticals ripped from the headlines. What should you do, for example, if your law firm "has concluded negotiations on behalf of a client in a North African country that is licensing information technology from a U.S.-based company and is finalising the terms of the agreement. The new government, elected following the pro-democracy revolution, is becoming increasingly frustrated with the anti-governmental demonstrations and is enacting measures to censor and restrict free speech and association."

The A4ID answer? "The firm will want to discuss with its client the evolving situation, the impact the political changes might have on the licensing arrangement, and the eventual ability of the client to operate without infringing on the rights of citizens." Regrettably, the guide does not tell you what to do if your client couldn't care less about the rights of citizens in a North African country and tells you to mind your own business.

Another example: A client with a refinery in Algeria asks you to review an employment contract for security personnel following an attack on its premises. A4ID advises that you "will not only want to review the contract in light of labour standards contained in key International Labour Organisation conventions, but also should consider whether the responsibilities assigned under the contract do not encourage excessive use of force by the security personnel that would result in infringements on the right to life of persons." Very careful, all this, but, you might think, a little flaccid.

What exactly is the "leverage" you as a lawyer are supposed to use to whip clients into line? Here are some of the tactics suggested by the guide. You could raise any issue of adverse human rights impacts.

You could suggest your firm can provide advice. You could advise on measures to avoid/mitigate/remedy adverse impacts. (Doing these things, of course, would add substantially to billable hours, and that's always welcome.) Your firm could also consider whether to decline or withdraw services, but, says the guide, "in practice, the firm is only likely to decline clients in exceptional circumstances and will more regularly try to use its leverage to mitigate the risk of human rights impacts once in an active client relationship."

All this is feeble stuff. And what world do the authors of the guide live in if they think this kind of dancing around is going to have any effect on hard-bitten businessmen operating overseas, often in a hostile environment, who demand down-to-earth advice from their outside counsel? This kind of discussion about international human rights might be okay in some obscure graduate seminar, but not in the boardrooms of, say, Canadian mining companies and their Bay Street law firms.

Oh yes, Canadian mining companies. They operate in places like Mexico, Guatemala, Peru, Zimbabwe, the Democratic Republic of the Congo, Tanzania, and Zambia, all of which countries, to say the least, are known to have local human rights issues. There's no evidence that their Canadian counsel are using "leverage" to promote the U.N. Guiding Principles. There is evidence that some of these companies are implicated in serious local human rights violations.

This past July, *Choc v. Hudbay Minerals* came out of left field. Justice Carole Brown ruled in Ontario Superior Court that lawsuits against Hudbay over alleged abuses at the company's Guatemalan project could proceed in Canada under Canadian law.* (The merits of the claims have yet to be determined.) Amnesty International, an intervenor, argued that Canadian courts should be able to draw upon international norms and standards of conduct, such as the UNGP, in assessing domestic liability for overseas human rights abuses.

The *Hudbay* decision, if it stands, could change the Canadian international human rights calculus. Companies and their counsel may be called to account, not in the courthouses of Guatemala

---

* The litigation was ongoing in 2017.

City and Kinshasa, but in Toronto and Vancouver. The U.N. Guiding Principles might suddenly become important.

But maybe we shouldn't get too excited. It was five years ago this past August that former Supreme Court of Canada Justice Ian Binnie told the Canadian Bar Association that Canadian businesses should pay attention to human rights abuses in Third World countries where they do business. No one was listening then. Perhaps no one is listening now.

DON'T BE RUDE
MARCH 2010

*"**Some think that the civility thing has gone too far.**" How rude can a lawyer be in the tough pursuit of his client's interests?*

Civility. Sometimes it seems the word is on every lawyer's lips.

Joe Groia has something to do with it. He's the Toronto lawyer who successfully defended John Felderhof, of Bre-X Minerals notoriety, on insider trading charges. Groia was said to have a "win at all costs" attitude at trial (he made the same complaint about the prosecution). He was accused of being strident and sarcastic, rude to the lawyer for the Ontario Securities Commission, and prone to "rhetorical excess" and "petulant invective." At one point, in convoluted proceedings that surrounded the Felderhof trial, Justice Marc Rosenberg of the Ontario Court of Appeal adopted the language of Justice Archie Campbell below who described Groia's trial conduct as "appallingly unrestrained and on occasion unprofessional."

Groia has become the poster-boy for incivility and is now the subject of disciplinary proceedings before Ontario's law society. Several of the law society's Rules of Professional Conduct bear on the civility issue. Rule 4.01(6), for example, requires a lawyer to be courteous and civil in the course of litigation; the commentary on the rule says, "A consistent pattern of rude, provocative, or disruptive conduct by the lawyer, even though unpunished as contempt, might well merit discipline." Despite formal exhortations like this, there's a growing feeling in the legal community that Groia has been treated unfairly, and that careful review of what actually happened shows that his conduct was not egregious. Some even think that this whole civility thing has gone too far.

Is it that Canadians like decorum and restraint, and object when someone raises his voice? Complaining about a lawyer's lack of civility smacks a little of whining to your mother because someone was mean to you in the schoolyard. But legal heavyweights say there is real substance to the problem. They say that incivility contributes to the complexity, cost and slowness of legal proceedings, and diminishes respect for the administration of justice. And the volume of complaints to law societies from the public about lack of professionalism by lawyers has accelerated dramatically in recent years. In Ontario, complaints about incivility, counseling or behaving dishonourably, and misleading the court, have increased from 11 per cent of all complaints in 2004, to 35 per cent in 2008.

Ontario leads on the civility issue, although most other provincial law societies, and the Canadian Bar Association, genuflect to the concept. (For example, a recent president of the B.C. law society wrote in a message to his members, with just a slight touch of xenophobia, "Civility and mutual respect are aspects of professionalism that need emphasis in these days of the portrayal of aggressive and preening lawyers on American television." The treasurer of Ontario's law society, Derry Millar, says, "The administration of justice depends upon the parties involved treating each other and the proceedings with respect." In recent months, Millar has orchestrated something called the Civility Forum, a series of meetings throughout Ontario supposed to provide an opportunity for members of the legal profession to discuss the importance of civility.

Those who are skeptical of the civility movement quickly point out the duty of a lawyer to be a zealous advocate for his client. The commentary on Ontario's Rule of Professional Conduct 4.01(1), about a lawyer's responsibility as advocate, says, "The lawyer has a duty to the client to raise fearlessly every issue, advance every argument, and ask every question, however distasteful, which the lawyer thinks will help the client's case…" Many lawyers believe fiercely that no holds are barred when representing someone, particularly in criminal matters and family law. Whenever I have suggested in these pages that sometimes a lawyer should back off, perhaps because of community standards that stand in the way of what he wants to do, I get lots of emails telling me that I just don't understand the job of an advocate. The commentary on Rule 4.01(1) goes on to say, "The lawyer must discharge this duty… in a manner that is consistent with the lawyer's duty to treat the tribunal with candour, fairness, courtesy…" Balancing these two apparently countervailing demands — zealous advocacy on the one hand, fairness and courtesy on the other — is the nub of the civility dilemma.

A couple of years ago, Alice Woolley, a law professor at the University of Calgary, published an article in the *Osgoode Hall Law Journal* challenging the civility movement. First of all, argues Woolley, excessive emphasis on professional courtesy and collegiality inhibits the search for truth about another lawyer's conduct. She writes: " The law of defamation still exists to give protection to lawyers who are unfairly subject to criticism by their colleagues. The addition of law society discipline fosters protectionism unnecessarily and suppresses legitimate criticism." More importantly, Woolley argues that the enforcement of good manners may obscure the real ethical principles at play. Often, for example, the focus should not be on whether a lawyer was rude, but on whether he was disloyal to the client or violated his duty to ensure the proper functioning of the legal system. Civility is not a proxy for these more fundamental considerations. Woolley concludes, "What is required is strong and cogent debate about how lawyers can be ethical… The civility movement should be abandoned in favour of this more difficult but ultimately more fruitful and important task." That is how she resolves the civility dilemma: Forget civility, and focus on what's underneath.

I'm with Professor Woolley. Fussing about politeness, as an end in itself, is silly. Sure, we should all be nice to each other, but it's not the end of the world if sometimes we're not, and sometimes we shouldn't be. On occasion, hard things need to be said to people who don't want to hear them. The picture of lawyers and judges getting together and chatting, delicately one presumes, about politeness in the law is faintly risible. Where is Monty Python when you need him? Okay, I better stop now, before I start getting really sarcastic.

SECRETS
SEPTEMBER 2008

"The basic rules now appear, well, hopelessly old-fashioned." In August 2008 Canada's privacy commissioner gave a speech to the Canadian Bar Association calling for better guidance for lawyers who are required to keep their clients information confidential. But what are lawyers to do in the age of teenage hackers and inept security by even the well heeled and the famous?

It's bewildering. We hear about the importance of privacy all the time, and there are a lot of rules supposed to protect personal information. Meanwhile, with modern technology, it has become easy to find out just about anything about just about anybody. Nothing seems safe any more. What's a lawyer, sitting on a mound of interesting and supposedly confidential information about his client and others, supposed to do in this complicated environment? What's the point of being discrete if anyone with an Internet connection (over 70 per cent of Canadians) can, legally or illicitly, find out what you know?

In the old days, the basic rules were straightforward enough and their application seemed simple. A lawyer could not divulge information acquired in the course of the professional relationship unless disclosure was authorized by the client or required by law. A lawyer wasn't even supposed to tell anyone the name of a client. Not even pillow talk was permissible. Human nature being what it is, there were — of course — egregious breaches of these old-fashioned strictures (particularly, one suspects, when it came to pillow talk).

Once I was in a crowded elevator with two lawyers from the same firm who went on and on about a file they were working on. Between street level and the seventh floor they pretty much gave their client's store away to a bunch of strangers. And not long ago, my wife and I were having dinner in a restaurant next to a party of lawyers loudly discussing litigation strategy in an important trial that I'd read about in the newspapers that morning. Oh, the frailty of human nature, particularly after a martini or two!

Anyway, it's a new world now. In a speech to this past August's Canadian Bar Association (CBA) annual meeting, Jennifer Stoddart, Canada's privacy commissioner, portentously described what she called the "radical transformation of the privacy landscape." Stoddart pointed out that Canadian law firms are subject to the *Personal Information Protection and Electronic Documents Act*, which establishes a variety of strict principles governing the collection, use and disclosure of personal information. She told the CBA that there was "a clear need for more practical guidance for lawyers" on privacy issues. The Privacy Commissioner's web site gives some help in its "legal corner." It all seems so complicated and confusing.

In her CBA speech, Stoddart also suggested that the "broad public" may not need to know the names and intimate personal details of individuals involved in litigation. The Internet, said Stoddart, spelled the end of "the concept of practical obscurity" which protected privacy *de facto*. Maybe, mused the Commissioner, initials could replace names in the reporting of cases. But this, like so much current chatter about privacy, is whistling past the graveyard. It is already widely accepted that the principle of open courts trumps privacy rights. The Supreme Court of Canada, and courts in several provinces, are actively considering posting court documents on line (with some thought to minimal privacy considerations, such as removing the names of minors). This has already happened in British Columbia, and is inevitable in other jurisdictions.

In September 2005, the Canadian Judicial Council (CJC), following a broad consultative process, published a model policy for access to court records. The policy endorsed the principle of openness and retained the presumption that all court records are available to the public at the courthouse. When technically feasible, said the CJC model policy, the public is also entitled to remote access to judgments and most docket information. And, increasingly, there are cameras in the courtroom. In 2007, in a pilot project, the Ontario Court of Appeal posted videos of more than 20 cases. Since 1997, the Cable Public Affairs Channel has carried regular broadcasts of Supreme Court of Canada hearings.

As usual, Canada is following the lead of the United States. In the September 2008 *Washington Lawyer* magazine, Sarah Kellogg reports that the U.S. Court of Appeals for the Seventh Circuit has a wiki, a web site that allows users to add or edit content, for its practitioner's handbook. "The court also uses RSS feeds, a messaging technology that notifies users when a blog or Web site has been updated, for audio postings of court arguments." A number of U.S. federal courts have similar programmes. And take a look at www.oyez.org, devoted to the U.S. Supreme Court; it will even tell you "where your favorite Justice is buried." Kellogg argues that, faced with these and other rapid developments, traditional legal journalism is rapidly disappearing. The same can also be said about traditional notions of privacy and confidentiality.

The basic rules now appear, well, hopelessly old-fashioned. They just don't seem to have much to do with reality. They don't respond to the avalanche of easily available information about everything. And, likewise, much contemporary rhetoric about privacy is beside the point. These days, anything goes. *The New York Times* reported recently that a computer hacker had broken into the e-mail account of Sarah Palin, and posted her messages and a list of her contacts on the Internet. The culprit turned out to be a 20-year-old student at the University of Tennessee, who said the whole thing was easy. He simply reset Palin's password using her birth date, ZIP code, and information about where she met her spouse, the security question on her Yahoo account, which he found on Google. You can read all about it on a *Wired* magazine blog called "Threat Level," which is devoted to chronicling privacy breaches. When you're finished with Threat Level, take a look at Wikileaks, whose motto is: "Have documents the world needs to see? We help you get the truth out." Wikileaks has a section devoted to Canada.

Canute the Great, a Viking king revered by his followers who thought him omnipotent, tried to demonstrate the limits of his authority by sitting on the beach and ordering the tide not to come in. "Let all men know how empty and worthless is the power of kings," he said following this experiment. Today one might say, let all men know how empty and worthless are the traditional notions of privacy and confidentiality.

BENDING THE RULES

TRUTH IN ADVERTISING

DECEMBER 2014

"Advertising has a lot to do with the legal profession's reality/ rhetoric disconnect." A law review article describes conflict between what lawyers representing clients accused of sexual offences say they do and professional codes of conduct. That dissonance is found in many areas of legal practice.

Do lawyers really do the highfalutin stuff they claim they do? Does the reality measure up to the rhetoric?

The rhetoric, in its purest form, is impressive (if just a little vague). The Canadian Judicial Council, for example, answering the question "what do lawyers do," says on its website, "Lawyers play a critical part in the justice system." A mediation website that I picked at random says, "Lawyers are agents of peace and order in the society." The United Nations has described lawyers as "essential agents of the administration of justice." Finding extravagant quotations of this kind is like shooting fish in a barrel. And, of course, woven through all the *ex cathedra* pronouncements is a lot of palaver about lawyers serving the public interest.

Pardon my cynicism, but I don't think very many lawyers show up for work in the morning thinking, "I'm an agent of peace, and today I will play a critical part in the justice system and also, while I'm at it, serve the public interest." (Although, they might make claims like these at a dinner party, after several glasses of wine). Along with everyone else in the work force, lawyers show up for work, often dispirited, with particular tasks to perform, tasks that are frequently dull and pedestrian. They also show up worried about whether they can cobble together six or seven billable hours for the day, fretting about where the next lot of clients and files are coming from, and wondering why their partners aren't pulling their weight.

One of the many criticisms leveled against my 2007 book *Lawyers Gone Bad* was that it was mostly about unprincipled solicitors and ignored the significant contribution to the justice system of other branches of the profession, particularly criminal defence lawyers. (I admit there was some merit to this criticism.) Criminal defence lawyers, so the argument goes, are wonderful people who selflessly fight for human rights, defend the innocent, protect the justice system, etc., etc. Eddie Greenspan, for example, has spoken eloquently and many times on this subject. He told the Empire Club as long ago as 1987, "Our community can retain justice and freedom only as long as it gives standing to one person to take, within the limits of the law, the defendant's side in court and to remind society when the scales of justice are tilting in the wrong direction." Great stuff.

But there's some reason to think that claims like these are more rhetoric than reality. Consider the recent paper by Elaine Craig of Dalhousie Law School, to be published soon in the *UBC Law Review*, called "Examining the Websites of Canada's 'Top Sex Crime Lawyers': The Ethical Parameters of Online Commercial Expression by the Criminal Defence Bar." The paper concludes, "A significant subset of lawyers who advertise legal representation services to individuals accused of sexual offences engage in commercial expression that may be inconsistent with the limits and guidelines specified in their professional codes of conduct." Craig analyzes defence lawyer websites that promote the acquittal of clients who appear to be factually guilty, trivialize sexual violence, and misstate the law or contain misleading and confusing legal information.

Advertising has a lot to do with the legal profession's reality/rhetoric disconnect. Lawyers should be free to advertise, but I understand why, for so long, provincial bars were reluctant to allow this to happen. Advertising encourages excess. For example, these days, if you ride the Toronto subway, you'll see advertisements for immigration lawyers. Posters in subway cars say things like, "Giving you and your family a happy life in Canada!" with pictures of parents hugging their kids. If a Toronto bus backs into you, as you fall to the ground you may notice an ad on the back of the bus featuring a smiling man in a suit, who happens to be a personal injury lawyer, extending his hand and offering you swift justice. The immigration and personal injury bars are important, for sure, but unregulated claims by them or any other lawyers lead to unrealistic expectations.

What about much-maligned business lawyers? You don't get much self-promoting flowery rhetoric from these guys. They don't often clamber up onto the soapbox and spout grandiloquent phrases. But they could, and they do have a story to tell. Here's how it goes: Business lawyers are the oil in the machine. They smooth the way for the operation of the vast capitalist system that creates wealth. They inject order and certainty into commerce, and help settle disputes that would otherwise be economically debilitating. Those who specialize in intellectual property promote and protect invention and ingenuity that we all benefit from. Even dull old property lawyers, busy registering titles, make it possible to borrow against real estate and thereby help unlock vast wealth that would otherwise be unproductive. And so on.

That's the rhetoric. The reality is somewhat different. As I've often said, business lawyers spend a lot of time helping the rich get richer. And, as Thomas Piketty has argued in his now-famous book, *Capital in the Twenty-First Century*, the rich are indeed getting spectacularly richer. There has never been greater inequality of wealth, with most increases coming from the deployment of capital rather than use of labour. Lawyers are small but important contributors to this regrettable development that bodes ill for society.

There's nothing wrong with high ideals, quite the contrary. They serve as our ethical lodestar. But reality is often brutal. We all have to be pragmatists. We all have to make a living. The trick is to reconcile the rhetoric and the reality, to operate effectively in a harsh world but not forget our bigger ethical purpose and obligations. That can be a very difficult balance to strike. But what choice do we have, if we want to be decent people and good lawyers?

ABETTING BAD BEHAVIOUR
APRIL 2012

"As Deep Throat said, if you want to understand how people behave, follow the money." There is rising concern that many of the professionals who help make unsavoury deals happen are lawyers, particularly in the world of mergers and acquisitions. Yet the lawyers are seldom held to account.

"The lawyer always goes home." This saying may seem a bit flippant or a trifle smug, but it captures an important point about the professional relationship between lawyer and client in the criminal justice system. If the client is a bad guy, he's the one who goes to jail, not the lawyer. The lawyer is not implicated in his client's crime, or tainted by it. He stands apart.

Maybe that's true in the criminal justice system, but it's not quite like that elsewhere in the legal world. Andrew Ross Sorkin of *The New York Times*, best-selling author of *Too Big to Fail*, recently wrote in his newspaper, "It increasingly seems that the lawyers aid and abet the bad behaviour of the nation's corporations, providing them with the cover of legal advice — sometimes knowingly, sometimes not."

Sorkin is particularly upset by "the utter lack of checkpoints put in place during a typical merger negotiation by an often seven-figure legal team." He gives as an example the recent $23 billion takeover of El Paso Corporation by Kinder Morgan. Goldman Sachs advised El Paso even though it owned 19.1 per cent of Kinder Morgan and had two representatives on that company's board. To make matters even worse (if that's possible), a Goldman Sachs banker who was advising El Paso on the transaction personally owned Kinder Morgan shares. None of the lawyers involved blew the whistle on these blatant conflicts of interest. Either they didn't know about them, which is virtually inconceivable, or they looked the other way and facilitated double-dealing. The law firms involved, by the way, were Wall Street heavyweights. Wachtell Lipton acted for El Paso, and Sullivan & Cromwell were the lawyers for Goldman Sachs. Sorkin concludes his article on this sad note: "For many years, if a lawyer was called 'commercial,' that was considered a pejorative. Today, it is increasingly a badge of honour."

In another recent article in *The New York Times*, Sorkin's colleague Joe Nocera wrote, "The kind of amoral, eat-what-you-kill capitalism that Goldman represents is one that most Americans instinctively find repugnant. It confirms the suspicions many people have that Wall Street has become a place where sleazy practices are the norm, and where generating profits in ways that are detrimental to society is the ticket to a successful career and a multimillion-dollar bonus." Nocera doesn't spell this out, but the sleazy practices of Goldman and the like are invariably aided and abetted by an army of professional lickspittles, particularly lawyers and accountants, anxious to do the bidding of their paymasters no matter where that might take them. This phenomenon is not, of course, confined to Wall Street. Hello Bay Street, The City of London, Nariman Point in Mumbai, La Défense in Paris, and the list goes on.

Here's where I have to stop and make quite clear that it would be unfair to tar all corporate lawyers with the same critical brush. Many are honourable and ethical. Many steer their clients firmly in the right direction. Some will resign from a file, or ditch a client, if they see a conflict or otherwise cannot square their conscience with what's going on. These ethical lawyers, bless them, do exist. But, regretfully, there are fewer and fewer. They are old school, and the old school is closing its doors for good.

Steven Harper (the other one) recently wrote in his acclaimed legal blog *The Belly of the Beast,* "Most big law firms have evolved — or devolved — into short-term bottom-line businesses." As that happens, to use Sorkin's words, the tag "commercial" becomes a badge of honour. The old-fashioned "I'm a professional" is supplanted by the modern "I'm a businessman."

Large and complex corporate transactions, particularly mergers and acquisitions involving public companies, are particularly fraught, with multiple interests easily in conflict. The chances are good that a big law firm advising one of the principal parties will also represent (or have represented in some other matter) a major shareholder or two (a pension fund, for instance), a commercial lender, a relevant government, one or more senior executives or board members of the companies involved, etc. etc. Sorting out and resolving these conflicts, some largely technical but others commercially real and important, is not an easy thing to do. The pressure within a law firm to ignore them is very powerful. To acknowledge these conflicts might involve walking away from a file or a client, and the commercial pressure not to take that costly step is enormous. For an individual lawyer it could mean waving goodbye to a bigger share of partnership profits and the promise of a highly successful career. As Deep Throat said, if you want to understand how people behave, follow the money.

About three years ago, as the economy collapsed around our ears, I wrote in these pages about the ethical responsibilities of lawyers in such circumstances. "If a lawyer, sitting in a conference room with his banker client, thinks that a mortgage applicant will soon default if given what he's asking for; or that a collateralized mortgage obligation is backed by loans that likely will collapse; or that a bond-rating agency hasn't done its homework and is handing out ratings that will mislead investors; or that financial engineering is going on that could have incalculable adverse consequences; he should stand up, put his hat on, and walk out." Predictably enough, some members of the profession criticized these views as naïve. Legal practice,

I was told, is morally neutral. A lawyer is not his brother's ethical keeper.

Presumably it is doubly naïve, in the world of so-called big law, to urge scrupulous regard for the niceties of conflicts. That's just not the way it is. It isn't commercial. And "commercial" is a badge of honour.

ETHICS AND THE YOUNG LAWYER
JUNE 2011

"Just because someone has been around a long time doesn't mean that he has a high ethical I.Q. or that his ethical sensibilities have been refined and honed by a long legal career." Is a lawyer ever too young or too junior to challenge the ethics of a well-established and powerful partner or employer?

Starting a legal career is daunting, whether you begin as big firm associate, member of a small partnership, solo practitioner, government lawyer or in-house counsel, whether you start out on Bay Street, in the burbs or on a country side-road.

Young lawyers worry about getting clients, billing enough hours, impressing their boss, paying the rent, building a reputation, developing expertise, having a future. Ethical issues don't appear nearly as pressing. If an ethical problem comes up, it seems natural and smart to defer to a senior lawyer in the firm or company, or to consult the law society, or ask some wise legal mentor. After all, if you're just starting out, what do you know?

But, deferring on ethical matters to a lawyer who sports the proverbial grey hair is not necessarily a good idea. Just because someone has been around a long time doesn't mean that he has a high ethical I.Q. or that his ethical sensibilities have been refined and honed by a long legal career. Quite the contrary, perhaps. Years on the battlefield may have taught a lawyer to be a brutal realist, to take no prisoners, to be ruthless in advancing his client's interests, to ignore what seem to be exquisite and pointless issues of right and wrong, not to be overly "academic" in his approach, to emphasize income rather than ethical sensibility. Innocence may have been lost a long time ago.

I don't think young lawyers should defer to their elders, or, if they do, they should be very careful about it. Here's a better idea for someone starting out. *Listen to your inner voice.* I know this sounds like trivial advice from a paperback bestseller or TV pop psychologist. But, although ethical issues can have a technical side (e.g., "How should this law society practice rule be interpreted?"), at bottom they are about applying our community's shared standards and morality and a common view of good sense. Those things are learned from family and friends, in school and at the hockey rink, from reading and private rumination. Every good citizen has a general sense of right and wrong.

Conflicts problems are an example. Lawyers know they must avoid conflicting interests in their practice, but what's a "conflicting interest?" To paraphrase Rule 2.04(1) of the Law Society of Upper Canada's Rules of Professional Conduct, a "conflicting interest" is an interest that would be likely to affect adversely a lawyer's judgment on behalf of, or loyalty to, a client or prospective client, or that a lawyer might be prompted to prefer to the interests of a client or prospective client. All provincial law societies have much the same practice rules about conflicts. There are lots and lots of these rules, and commentaries on them, and, of course, cases (most notably the 2002 Supreme Court of Canada decision in *R. v. Neil*). It's not long before we're spinning intricate webs of legal rhetoric, but the rhetoric is likely to be confusing if not misleading. Most times, left to his own devices, the sensible lawyer will instinctively recognize a conflict of interest and doesn't need theory to do so. U.S. Supreme Court Justice Potter Stewart said in *Jacobellis v. Ohio* (1964), about hardcore pornography, that he couldn't define it but "I know it when I see it." It's the same with conflicts.

A youngish lawyer told me the following story. His large firm represented a public company and, separately, the CEO and chairman of that company who was also a substantial shareholder. The company got into financial difficulty through bad management and needed to be reorganized to survive, a reorganization that would inflict pain on shareholders. My youngish friend went to the senior partner who acted for both the company and the CEO, and inquired how it was possible, in these circumstances, to act for both, since there seemed to be clearly conflicting interests. "It's as if there is a building with two entrance doors," said the senior partner, determined to hang on to both clients. "Two doors, yes, but each door opens into the same building." My friend wasn't buying this mysterious metaphor: he knew a conflict when he saw it, and, at some cost to his career within the firm, pursued the issue until the firm's executive committee decided that one of the two clients had to go. What mattered was gut instinct, not fancy reasoning. What often makes conflicts issues like these so troublesome is that ethical and business demands clash. Faced with what might be a conflict, the right thing may be to refuse a potential client or send an existing one to another lawyer, but that means losing revenue which is a tough thing to do.

The ethics/business dilemma is not restricted to conflicts; it is pervasive in the practice of law. Mark Everson recently published a poignant op-ed piece in *The New York Times*. Everson, an accountant and former commissioner of the U.S. Internal Revenue Service, wrote that once "the mission of the junior accountant or lawyer was clear to all: help clients adhere to professional standards and follow the law." Now, he says, accountants and lawyers "see their practices not as independent firms that strengthen the integrity of capitalism, but as businesses measured chiefly by the earnings of their partners." Everson suggests that this ethical sea change throws into doubt such fundamental concepts as attorney-client privilege as it applies to corporations.

Ethical considerations often pull one way, business interests another. That's the biggest problem that most young lawyers will have to face, and the advice of senior lawyers may not be reliable in this matter. So, I come back to my general point: *listen to your inner voice.* Have faith in your personal ethical instincts, and be suspicious of what legal sophisticates may present as the way of the world. Ethics is a deeply personal business, and you're as good a judge — maybe better — than anyone else.

IN FOR A PENNY, IN FOR A POUND
JANUARY 2010

"Is there a difference, if you're broke, between borrowing for food and shelter, say, versus a winter holiday in the sun?" In late 2009 a case before the U.S. Supreme Court raised the issue of whether a law firm could counsel a client facing bankruptcy to take on more debt. Does the purpose of the new debt matter?

Is it ethical for a lawyer to advise a client considering bankruptcy to incur more debt? After all, if the client is insolvent, any new debt will likely not be fully repaid, and will dilute existing creditors. Does it matter what the debt is for? Is there a difference, if you're broke, between borrowing for food and shelter, say, versus a winter holiday in the sun?

The United States Supreme Court is currently considering these difficult issues. The U.S. *Bankruptcy Abuse Prevention and Consumer Protection Act* (BAPCPA) prohibits debt relief agencies, which arguably includes lawyers, from advising a client to incur more debt in contemplation of bankruptcy. In *Milavetz, Gallop & Milavetz v. United States*, heard by the Supreme Court in December 2009, a Minnesota law firm argued that they either had to violate their ethical obligations under the Minnesota Rules of Professional Conduct to give clients "appropriate and beneficial advice," or be in breach of BAPCPA; this, they said, put them, and every other lawyer, in an impossible position. The American Bar Association supported the plaintiffs, and argued that, if BAPCPA applied to attorneys, it would interfere with regulation of the legal profession by state judicial systems, and with the ability of attorneys to advise clients in financial distress. The Supreme Court judgment in Milavetz is not expected until sometime in 2011.*

Questions and comments from the bench in Milavetz were vigorous and animated. Many of the justices seemed to enjoy toying with ethical dilemmas. Justice Sotomayor asked: Can it ever be ethical for a lawyer to do something illegal? Is there a difference between unethical and illegal advice? Justice Ginsburg wondered whether advising a client contemplating bankruptcy to take on more debt was okay in some circumstances — if money were needed to treat serious cancer, for example. Justice Alito commented, "If a person takes on additional debt in order to obtain life-saving treatment, that is not done in contemplation of bankruptcy... It's done because there is an emergency that requires immediate expenditures." Justice Antonin Scalia, in his inimitable fashion, was much less nuanced. "It's a stupid law," he said of BAPCPA, adding, to laughter in the courtroom, "Where is the prohibition of stupid laws in the Constitution?"

I know of no explicit law in Canada forbidding a lawyer or anyone else from suggesting to someone contemplating bankruptcy that he or she take on more debt. The federal *Bankruptcy and Insolvency Act* does not address the issue. Provincial fraudulent conveyance legislation only provides for the setting aside of improper transfers of property. Counseling fraud is an offence under the *Criminal Code*, but in most cases taking on additional debt when considering bankruptcy does not amount to criminal fraud.

What about ethical rules set out by provincial law societies? They don't help. The Law Society of Ontario's Rules of Professional Conduct has nothing directly on point, although I suppose some rules might apply tangentially — for example, 2.02(5), which says, "When advising a client, a lawyer shall not knowingly assist in or encourage any dishonesty, fraud, crime, or illegal conduct, or instruct

---

*The U.S. Supreme Court decided that BAPCPA prohibited only advice that a client incur more debt *because* the client intends to file for bankruptcy protection.

the client on how to violate the law and avoid punishment." The Law Society of British Columbia Professional Conduct Handbook is a bit more to the point: Paragraph 6, chapter 4, says, "A lawyer must not engage in any activity that the lawyer knows or ought to know assists in or encourages any dishonesty, crime or fraud, including a fraudulent conveyance, preference or settlement." The Nova Scotia Barristers' Society Legal Ethics Handbook, commentary 21.3, contains the usual bromide: "The lawyer has a duty not to subvert the law by counseling or assisting in activities which are in defiance of it and has a duty not to do anything to lessen the respect and confidence of the public in the legal system of which the lawyer is a part."

There's a lot of tricky issues here. Go back for a minute to the questioning of Milavetz counsel by the U.S. Supreme Court justices. Justice Alito asked, "Well, let's say someone goes to the lawyer and they discuss the person's debt situation and the decision is made that a bankruptcy petition is going to be filed at some future date. Do you think that everything that person does after that point is done in contemplation of bankruptcy?" Chief Justice Roberts wondered what a lawyer should say if asked by a client, "I know we are thinking of filing bankruptcy, but I want to go to Tahiti and charge it; can I do it?" Later the chief justice added: "What if the person takes a trip to Tahiti every November? They've always done it. They are not intending to defraud the debtor. They are just doing what they have always done." Justice Ginsburg inquired what the lawyer could tell the client about paying legal fees. Asked Justice Sotomayor: "How about the person comes in, shows the attorney his or her financial state. There is no money to pay the fee. The attorney simply gives a bill and says, 'I need it by Friday.'"

How does a Canadian lawyer deal with problems like these, in the absence of formal legal and ethical requirements? Feeble as it sounds, I think he or she has to fall back on a sense of what the society they work in regards as right and wrong (often not an easy thing to figure out). Most people in this country would probably consider it wrong to advise or help a client contemplating bankruptcy to incur more debt, save in the most dire of circumstances. That doesn't mean, of course, that a client can't be told that it may be lawful to do so.

Whenever I suggest in these pages that community morality should have a role in determining legal advice, I get emails telling me that I just don't understand what being a lawyer is all about. My inbox is waiting.

TRUTH FOR SALE

NOVEMBER 2009

"Even if you embrace the hired gun theory, surely not everything and anything is OK. Where and how do you draw the line?" The so-called U.S. "torture memos," about the legality of using torture to interrogate terrorism suspects, were written by lawyers between 2002 and 2007. Traditionally, legal opinions are the essence of good lawyering, a legal way to find a path for clients. Has that changed?

A formal legal opinion, properly done, is the essence of lawyering. It sorts out the relevant facts. It marshals the appropriate law. It contains a dollop or two of common sense and a measure of worldly experience. From this brew comes the "opinion" itself, a well-considered, amply supported legal conclusion that commands respect and can be relied on by the client who asked (and generally paid) for it. It is ethically inspired and seeks the truth so far as it can be found. It is professionalism at its best. This is what we lawyers aspire to. Or do we?

Some skeptics think the legal opinion has become just another commodity, tailored to the needs of the consumer, bought and sold in a competitive marketplace like any other product. Regard for ethics and the legal truth, these critics say, has been lost. Exhibit A for this point of view is the so-called "torture memos," a series of legal opinions written between 2002 and 2007 by lawyers in the Office of

Legal Counsel (OLC) at the United States Department of Justice, all justifying a wide variety of Central Intelligence Agency techniques used in interrogating al-Qaeda suspects. The techniques included menacing a suspect with a power drill, and threatening to rape his mother and kill his children. All of these techniques were legal, said the memos, most of which can now be seen on a variety of websites, including that of the American Civil Liberties Union.

Writing in *The New York Review of Books*, David Cole, a professor at Georgetown law school in Washington, DC, says of the torture memos that they "reveal a sustained effort by OLC lawyers to rationalize a predetermined and illegal result." Cole writes, "Law at its worst treats legal doctrine as infinitely manipulable, capable of being twisted cynically in whatever direction serves the client's desires." The authors of the memos were not low-level functionaries who could only be expected to do what they were told, and didn't understand the significance of what they were about. They included Jay Bybee, an assistant attorney general and now a federal judge on the U.S. Court of Appeals for the Ninth Circuit, and John Yoo, a deputy assistant attorney general and former clerk for Justice Clarence Thomas, now a law professor at Berkeley.

I can hear the reader mumbling: Just a minute, what are you going on about? Writing U.S. legal opinions justifying torture is a world away from what happens in law offices on Toronto's Bay Street, or in those on 13th Street in Prince Albert, Saskatchewan, or — come to that — in the Justice Department building on Wellington Street in Ottawa. But, in law offices across Canada, every day, legal opinions on a vast variety of questions are being carefully crafted to meet a client's needs and desires. Most of them are noncontroversial and entirely innocuous, dealing with routine matters. But some are not. Some sail close to the wind. They might bless doubtful tax shelters, for example. They might sanction employer contribution holidays from defined benefit pension plans. They might approve huge retention bonuses for senior executives of a company in serious financial difficulty.

But there are no Canadian "torture memos," right? If only that were true. The Canadian Press reports that in December, 2005 the

Canadian Justice Department gave a 10-page opinion to the Foreign Affairs Department that "extraordinary rendition," the U.S. practice of shipping terrorism suspects to foreign prisons where harsh interrogation techniques are used (remember Maher Arar?), was lawful in some circumstances. Extraordinary rendition is sometimes called "torture by proxy." So far as I can discover, the text of this Canadian government legal opinion has not been made public. It should be. We need to know what it says.

When I practised law as a partner in a big firm, I told junior lawyers, echoing the party line, that our job was to find a lawful way for clients to do whatever they wanted. There was almost always a path to the desired result, I said, provided we were imaginative and clever. The law is so complex and difficult that it permits a wide variety of plausible interpretations, including ones that completely contradict each other. So, let's find the right answer — the one the client wants — and be prepared to write an opinion that says everything is fine. Anything is legally possible, if we lawyers try hard enough; that's why clients pay us, and pay us well.

Is it okay for lawyers to be just guns for hire? Or should legal practice, including the giving of legal opinions, be underpinned and constrained by commitment to personal and social ethical standards? I was lambasted a few months ago for arguing in these pages that lawyers should take into account the values and well being of their community. A lawyer's job, my bad tempered critics said, is to represent the client, any client, to the utmost, no matter what, without allowing particular ethical considerations (which may not be universally shared) to muddle things up and get in the way. Our very system of justice, they told me, the entire adversarial system, etc., etc., depends on it.

Maybe, but surely a line has to be drawn somewhere. Even if you embrace the hired gun theory, surely not everything and anything is okay. Where and how do you draw the line? Torture memos? Most lawyers, I believe, would say that such opinions are not acceptable, but Judge Bybee, Professor Yoo, and perhaps some lawyers in the Canadian Department of Justice, thought differently. Aggressive tax shelter opinions, helping the rich get richer and depriving the public treasury of funds needed for great public projects? That's more difficult; most would think that such opinions are just part of a normal day's work, but a very senior tax lawyer of my acquaintance, impressively, would have nothing to do with them on ethical grounds. Good for him.

LOST TO AMBITION
AUGUST 2009

"Often, the most successful lawyer resents the success of his fellows. Many solicitors envy the riches of their clients. Who in a big firm has not felt unappreciated?" In late 2008, a U.S. lawyer who had been stealing from his clients for years was finally caught when he attempted to execute one of his frauds in a Toronto boardroom. His sentencing letter was enlightening about the temptations faced by many lawyers everyday.

"I have betrayed the people I care about the most, and I suffer every day from… shame and self-loathing and regret…"

So wrote disgraced New York lawyer Marc Dreier, after pleading guilty to massive fraud, in his sentencing letter to Judge Jed Rakoff of the Federal District Court in Manhattan. Dreier composed the letter to give "some context to what I did… to explain how a person with my background and advantages came to do the unconscionable." A legal website called Dreier's frauds "the most brazen and spectacular deception in law firm history." His sentencing letter unexpectedly tells us something important about the ethical perils of legal practice.

When the roof fell in, Dreier, in his late fifties, had a $10 million Manhattan condominium, a waterfront home in the Hamptons, a house in Santa Monica, California, a home in Anguilla, a $40 million art collection, and an $18 million yacht with a permanent crew of ten (including a chef). Divorced with two children, he had dated a succession of beautiful young women. A graduate of Yale and Harvard law school, he was the sole owner of a New York based law firm, Dreier LLP, with 250 employees. Today, tagged the "Houdini of impersonation" by the popular press, Marc Dreier is in prison.

The final act in this sorry saga took place in Canada. On December 2, 2008, Drier flew from New York to Toronto by private jet and went to the Ontario Teachers' Pension Plan offices. After meeting with Michael Padfield, a lawyer for Teachers, Dreier asked to use a telephone and was shown into a conference room. There he met with Howard Steinberg, a New York hedge fund representative he had previously invited to the Teachers' offices. Dreier pretended he was Padfield, used Padfield's business card (that he'd been given earlier), and tried to close the sale to the hedge fund of $33 million in fraudulent promissory notes supposedly backed by Teachers.

Steinberg sensed something was wrong, and ended the meeting early. He asked a receptionist if the man who had just left the conference room was Michael Padfield, and was told that he wasn't. Police were called. Dreier was arrested. Later it turned out that Dreier had defrauded a variety of investors of hundreds of millions of dollars; often, as part of the deception, he had impersonated someone. In July, he pleaded guilty to multiple counts of fraud, and Judge Rakoff sent him to jail for 20 years.

It's easy to see this story as the usual titillating morality tale of excess, greed, and venality. It is tempting to dismiss Marc Dreier as an almost comic figure, a Bernie Madoff lite, someone whose story is not worth thinking about once we have slaked our thirst for the sensational. But I think it worth pausing for a moment or two over Dreier's sentencing letter. Letters like these are generally self-serving in the extreme, the last desperate pitch of a criminal, but Dreier's is poignant and seems honest. It suggests a classic tragedy — a man brought to ruin as a consequence of a tragic flaw, moral weakness, or inability to cope with unfavourable circumstances.

In the letter, Dreier described his first 20 years in legal practice, as an associate and then partner with prominent New York law firms. His account will seem familiar to many lawyers. "I performed well,"

Dreier wrote, "but I was achieving less satisfaction and recognition than I expected. Colleagues of mine and certainly clients of mine were doing much better financially and seemingly enjoyed more status. By my mid-forties I felt crushed by a sense of underachievement."

In 1996, in his mid-forties, Dreier did what many dissatisfied big firm lawyers do: he started his own law firm. But, he wrote, he planned poorly, particularly for expenses. By 2001, he was deeply in debt. In 2002, an expensive divorce made things worse. "All of this left me feeling overwhelmed — by my debt, by a disappointing career, by a failed marriage." Dreier started stealing, initially to service law firm debt and fund the firm's expansion. "I was desperate for some measure of the success that I felt had eluded me. I felt that my law firm was my last chance to make a mark for myself, and I was fearful of seeing it fail." Later, inevitably, Dreier used some of the money he'd stolen to buy the houses, yacht, art, expensive cars and other luxuries.

By his own account, Dreier was driven by the desire, familiar to many of us, to succeed in a highly visible way. The trappings of wealth were essential, for they told the story he wanted the world to know; after all, what good is success, unless everyone can see it? He fell easily into the trap of starting his own eponymous firm, a place where by design his personal stature and achievement would be fully recognized. And, like many lawyers, he was a poor businessperson, unable to balance the books honestly, perennially teetering on the economic brink.

Marc Dreier's crookedness and braggadocio are highly unusual (although not unique). Nonetheless, many straight-shooting lawyers might recognize something of Dreier in themselves. Often the most successful lawyer resents the success of his fellows. Many solicitors envy the riches of their clients. Who in a big firm has not felt unappreciated? What unappreciated big firm lawyer has not dreamt of starting his own firm? And it is often observed that the smartest lawyer can be the dumbest businessperson, unable — among other things — to get a grip on the expense side of the ledger.

The Dreier sentencing letter ends on a poignant note. "My whole ambition in life was to be a lawyer who would distinguish himself… I lost myself to my ambition and sacrificed everything else…. I have lost everything a man can lose."

A tragedy, I think, and a cautionary tale as well.

WHEN IS A CONTRACT NOT A CONTRACT?

APRIL 2009

"Now, a contract may or may not be respected and performed by the parties — it all depends." As companies and countries swayed and buckled under the ravages of collapsing markets in the aftermath of the 2008 financial crisis, many asked why the architects of the disaster continued to collect huge bonuses under their employment contracts. Contract law, many said, needs to change.

Contracts are sacrosanct.

This principle has been pounded into law students' heads since legal education began. Professors pontificate as follows: provided certain formalities are met, and public policy is not offended, individuals (including juridical persons, corporations being the most important of these) are free to create private law between themselves. If necessary, courts will enforce this private law. Our freedom, our economy — gosh, our very way of life — depend upon this being so. (Full disclosure — I taught the law of contracts over many years in several law schools, and always toed this traditional line.)

Until fairly recently, law graduates have reverently carried the principle of *pacta sunt servanda* into the practice of law. Clients beyond count have been told that the terms of a contract are mighty important. Sign nothing, they have been instructed, until you have read and agreed with every word. Once you have agreed, you will be bound to do what you have promised; you'll be punished if you don't. In my two decades of legal practice, I always dutifully said all of this. After all, we advocates intoned dolefully, respect for contracts is the rock upon which our society is built. It was only after I left the law that I decided the whole contract thing was overrated, and was prepared to sign just about anything if I liked and trusted the person on the other side. But that's another story…

Now, we are suffering a sea change. Prompted by the corrosive effect of the current economic climate, traditional ethical precepts about the law of contract are being tossed out the window. *The New York Times* lately published an article with the headline, "Contracts Now Seen as Being Rewritable." The article began, "Contracts everywhere are under assault." Employment contracts are thought to be particularly vulnerable, but other types of agreements may also be in doubt. For example, U.S. Treasury Secretary Geitner is apparently working on an initiative to give the federal government wide power to modify the contracts of financial institutions it takes over.

The flashpoint for the collapse of contract seems to have been the $165 million in bonuses promised and paid to senior executives of AIG, the insurance giant that was run into the ground by the very same executives who collected the bonus money. The AIG collapse famously almost took down the world financial system, and the company had to be rescued by the American government to the tune of $170 billion. President Obama said the employment contracts in question should be torn up. "This isn't just a matter of dollars and cents," the president said. "It's about our fundamental values."

The battle lines were quickly drawn following Obama's angry comment. Andrew Ross Sorkin, mergers and acquisitions columnist for *The New York Times*, wrote that Wall Street types agreed with the president that fundamental values had to be respected, "but from their point of view, the 'fundamental value' in question here is the sanctity of contract." Professor Lawrence Cunningham of George Washington University Law School opined in the same newspaper, "moral outrage and public rebuke do not provide legal grounds for backing out of a contract."

But Professor Cunningham, apparently a stealth anti-contract operative, then went on to list all the perfectly acceptable legal reasons for repudiating the terms of an agreement. "Our legal and business system," he wrote, "recognizes plenty of valid excuses from contractual duty and even justification for breaching." These excuses include aggressive and creative interpretation of the contract itself, misconduct or fraud by the other side, the effect of unforeseeable or uncontrollable circumstances (so-called *force majeure*), and the possibility of a fraudulent conveyance. And, as any practising lawyer knows, often just the *allegation* of these things roils the waters enough to make an inconvenient contract go away, particularly if you're Goliath to somebody else's David.

Bankruptcy protection is the ultimate contract-buster for a company in trouble. In Canada, this protection is generally obtained by filing under the federal *Companies' Creditors Arrangement Act* (CCAA). Such a filing produces a court order giving the company pretty-much blanket immunity, for a time, from its creditors, which includes suppliers and employees. Major companies — Nortel, Abitibi-Bowater — have filed for CCAA protection, and others are expected to do so soon. When this happens, folks, tear up those contracts you were relying on! Now they're just words on a piece of paper, signifying nothing.

And so, the old-fashioned view that, as an ethical matter, lawyers should not advise clients to break contracts, and shouldn't figure out good ways for them to ignore commitments presumed binding, is just that — an old-fashioned view, no longer relevant, out of tune with the times. Now, a contract may or may not be respected and performed by the parties — it all depends. That's the correct legal advice. This is another example of morally neutral lawyering, the belief that lawyers are there to serve clients and it's not their business to protect society or promote particular values at a client's expense. (I have recently argued in this column that a lawyer's moral neutrality, desirable as it may be in some ways, doesn't mean that he is free to subvert the values of his society, or be blind to its best interests. Even law society rules make this clear. Not everyone agrees.)

Back to those pontificating law professors. I think the time has come for them to rejig the basic law of contract course, taught everywhere in first year. Students should now be told that a contract is just one tentative way of organizing your affairs. You may think you have enforceable private law rights, but don't count on it; they can disappear as do the snows of winter (except a lot faster). And, if you're on the other side, don't worry too much about obligations that have become burdensome; there are plenty of ways out. As for lawyers? We're here to help.

ACCESS TO JUSTICE

FIGHTING FOR US
JANUARY 2017

"It's time the legal profession formed coalitions to fight for big principles on behalf of all the people. Access to justice would be a good place to start." Several top U.S. law firms formed a coalition in 2016 to fight for gun control following horrific mass shootings that targeted highly vulnerable people, including kindergarten children and nightclub goers.

How can the legal profession mobilize for the public good? Lawyers shouldn't just fight for particular and partisan interests. Sometimes they should struggle for the big things, for overarching principles. Instead of fighting each other, they should stand together and fight for the people. It's an ethical imperative.

Pollyannaish, you think? Never going to happen? You might be wrong about that if a surprising recent event in the United States is anything to go by. *The New York Times* reported in December that several of the biggest and most powerful law firms in America have formed a coalition to fight for gun control. The group includes such pillars of the legal establishment as Paul Weiss Rifkind Wharton & Garrison, Covington & Burling, Dentons, O'Melveny & Myers, Hogan Lovells, and Arnold & Porter. *The Times* said the coalition was "the first time in decades that rival corporate law firms, more accustomed to beating back regulation than championing it, have joined forces to file litigation nationwide around such a polarizing social issue as guns. The effort harks back to the civil rights era, when President John F. Kennedy summoned 250 top lawyers to the White House and enlisted their help in fighting segregation."

To do this takes *cojones*. Each of these law firms has clients involved with the gun industry and sympathetic to the National Rifle Association. Any advocacy for gun control will offend the many hard line supporters of the U.S. Constitution's Second Amendment ("A well regulated Militia, being necessary to the security of a free State, the right of the people to keep and bear Arms, shall not be infringed.") President Trump, who has promised to defend the Second Amendment, may not find the coalition amusing. He may even tweet about it. But, as Brad S. Karp, chairman of Paul Weiss, said after the June 2016 Orlando nightclub shooting, "It is in our DNA to act when we see injustice."

The gun control coalition intends to pursue multi-pronged lines of attack. It will challenge state laws "that arguably force citizens and local governments to allow guns to be carried on their properties, including schools, airports, shopping malls and bars." It will attack the restriction on the Bureau of Alcohol, Tobacco, Firearms and Explosives from releasing data about the use of firearms in crimes. It will pursue the gun industry for antitrust violations on the basis that some gun companies have joined forces to limit the development of safety technology. These are only some of the initiatives the coalition is planning. This transcendent and unexpected development will go a long way towards restoring faith in the tarnished reputation of the U.S. legal profession.

What about Canada? It's hard to find evidence that the legal establishment of this country is prepared to lay it on the line in a co-ordinated effort to promote the public good. Scattered and anaemic *pro bono* programs, and the occasional heroic individual effort, just don't cut it. But maybe now, inspired by the American example, the time has finally come. So listen up, so-called Seven Sisters, and other law firms that aspire to join the pantheon (you know who you are). It's time to form a coalition.

A coalition for what? There is no shortage of issues in Canada that would benefit greatly from concerted legal attention. Three are obvious. The first is access to justice. From Chief Justice Beverley McLachlin on down, everyone knows that the Canadian justice system is crippled, unavailable to most ordinary Canadians, no matter the need, because of the cost (the Chief Justice has often spoken eloquently about this appalling situation). Second, there is the complex plight of Canada's indigenous peoples. For years this situation has been a big and spreading stain on the country's escutcheon. And finally there is the state of the environment, which becomes more and more frightening as we lurch towards an almost certain ecological disaster that will overtake our children and grandchildren if we don't take quick and dramatic action.

There can, of course, be more than one legal coalition. The coalition idea might be a whole new way of simultaneously addressing many of the big problems that plague us. And it might help repurpose and redraw the legal profession, giving it its rightful role, turning it from a tired, old, traditional, business enterprise into a pioneer for justice and a leader of society. Wouldn't that be swell?

Any of the complex problems I mention will be extraordinarily difficult to address effectively. To do so will require agreement on contentious issues, a carefully crafted plan, clever and committed lawyers, a lot of money, and some self-sacrifice. Above all it will require leadership of unquestioned credibility and experience.

Access to justice should be the first issue to be addressed by a legal coalition. It's a well-understood problem. Its contours are clear. It is particularly the domain of lawyers (in some ways, very limited access to justice is a problem they have created and therefore own). It is fixable, albeit at some financial and other cost to the legal profession itself.

There are a number of impressive people who could lead a legal coalition to deal with the access to justice problem. Two in particular come to mind. As it happens, both will be out of work soon and may be looking for something to do. David Johnston's term as Governor General ends this September. He is a lawyer and former law dean and university president. He is used to moving confidently among the influential and powerful, and forging consensus. He has carefully-considered views on the problem. Take a look at his excellent 2011 speech to the Canadian Bar Association which, of course, the profession largely ignored.

And then there's Beverley McLachlin. She must retire from the Supreme Court of Canada by September 2018.* There is wide, virtually unparalleled, respect for her person and career. She is obviously deeply troubled by the access to justice issue.

Help us!

---

*In June 2017 Chief Justice McLachlin announced she would retire on December 15.

DEFENDING THE INDEFENSIBLE
APRIL 2015

"Several judges were outraged by Freedman's arguments and sought unsuccessfully to have him disbarred and fired from his teaching position." In February 2015 legal ethics writer and gadfly Monroe Freedman died. He was an influential law professor and writer who argued that legal representation includes the client's right to full confidentiality, even when perjury was involved.

Monroe Freedman died in February.

I can hear you asking: "Who on earth was Monroe Freedman?"

The New York Times described him in a lengthy obituary as "a dominant figure in legal ethics whose work helped chart the course of lawyers' behaviour in the late 20th century and beyond…"

That's who he was.

Freedman's fame rests mostly on his book *Understanding Lawyers' Ethics*. His core belief was that every citizen is entitled to justice. He thought that the principal ethical responsibility of a lawyer is to do everything possible to promote access to justice. Sometimes, Freedman argued, this fundamental obligation will lead to unexpected conclusions. Is advertising by lawyers okay? Yes: That's how members of society most in need of information find out about their legal rights. What about chasing ambulances? That's okay too: Chasing ambulances is another way of alerting people to their legal entitlements.

Freedman's most famous pronouncement, made in a 1966 lecture, was about what a lawyer should do if he knows that a client in a criminal trial intends to perjure himself. The lecture was published in the *Michigan Law Review*. Freedman said that a lawyer should make all possible efforts to dissuade his client from lying on the stand, but, if he fails and perjury is committed, he should say nothing. And, more than that, Freedman argued that in some instances "I t is proper to give your client legal advice when you have reason to believe that the knowledge you give him will tempt him to commit perjury."

Part of a lawyer's obligation to keep quiet about perjury, thought Freedman, comes from a client's entitlement to confidentiality. Confidentiality, in the adversary system, "allows the attorney no alternative to putting a perjurious witness on the stand without explicit or implicit disclosure of the attorney's knowledge to either the judge or the jury." Even more important is the broad context of the justice system. Only the lawyer stands between the criminal defendant and the unlimited resources of government. He has a moral duty of loyalty to his client. He is the champion of someone confronting overwhelming power. And, as a matter of moral principle, you cannot criticize a lawyer for actions taken in a representative capacity.

Several judges, including then-federal appeals judge Warren Burger, later chief justice of the United States, were outraged by Freedman's arguments and sought unsuccessfully to have him disbarred and fired from his teaching position at Hofstra University. Freedman knew how to hold a grudge. He never forgot or forgave Burger's attack, and took every opportunity in his published work to cite judgments of the Chief Justice as illustrations of legal error.

Burger has long-since passed into the corridors of obscure legal history, but almost 50 years on the Freedman lecture remains influential. Its lasting merit is that it makes you think about important but subtle issues of law and ethics, and punctures stultified and conventional thinking. It makes you consider afresh, for example, a criminal defence lawyer's responsibility when he knows or strongly suspects that his client is guilty.

Freedman is robust on a lawyer's responsibility to represent his client fearlessly. Some say this is an American point-of-view, different from the British and Canadian cautious approach that emphasizes a lawyer's duty to the court, a duty that must be respected even to the detriment of a client's interests. The strict and cautious view is well summed up in the Advocates Society's *Principles of Civility* that warns, "Advocates cannot condone the use of perjured evidence and, if they become aware of perjury at any time, they must immediately seek the client's consent to bring it to the attention of the court. Failing that, advocates must withdraw."

I asked two prominent and highly experienced Toronto litigators, both long-time benchers of the Law Society: What would you do if it was clear your client was going to perjure himself? Both seemed uneasy with the question. Neither fell back on the Advocates Society's *Principles of Civility*. One emailed, "I was taught that if you have (and keep) a client who you know will commit perjury on the stand, you can put him on the stand, but only ask him to tell his story when he gets on the stand. ... Depending on the timing, the best course is to explain your constraints, at which point the client will likely retain someone else who is not so constrained." The other said, "Boy, that's a problem, that would be a mess." After a moment's reflection, he added, "I think you'd have to withdraw."

Monroe Freedman was ever the gadfly, sometimes humorous, sometimes cranky, often eccentric, increasingly gloomy. (Interestingly, his on-line student ratings are very poor, among the worst I've ever seen.) In 2013, still going strong, he commented on the Edward Snowden affair in a paper called "Our Inalienable Rights Can Never Be Recovered." Wrote Freedman: "We live in a Surveillance State in a Surveillance World. It is ever expanding and omnipresent. It can never be removed or restricted, and our Constitution, with its Bill of Rights and separation of powers, has been lost forever."

In October 2014, Freedman and his granddaughter handed out opera lyrics outside Lincoln Center in Manhattan to protest the Metropolitan Opera's production of *The Death of Klinghoffer*. Freedman said the libretto contained passages similar to the language used by Hitler's propaganda minister Joseph Goebbels. He once told students, "As you contemplate the practice of law, you should under-stand that you may be called upon to represent people who, out of sheer greed, will hurt and even kill other innocent people. And if you can't handle that then you should not go into the practice of corpor-ate law." And he was a member of the Flat Earth Society.

Let us celebrate the gadfly! RIP, Monroe Freedman.

OPEN TO ALL: THE LEGAL SYSTEM AND THE RITZ HOTEL

FEBRUARY 2012

"The biggest ethical problem for lawyers of them all. The fact that most Canadians cannot use the law and legal system that we once thought belonged to all who live in this country." In 2009 the median after-tax income for Canadian families was $63,800. For senior families, it was $46,800. These are only medians, and plenty of families were living on less. While many eminent lawyers decry the unavailability of legal services, including the chief justice of Canada, nothing is done to address the problem.

The Saskatchewan Crown Counsel Association recently invited me to come to Regina and speak to government lawyers about ethical and professional issues. It was an honour to be asked, and I was happy to accept, but I wondered, what should I talk about?

Often a discussion of "ethical and professional issues" is a dry dissection of the latest on solicitor-client privilege, or conflicts of interest, or some other quotidian problem that faces the individual lawyer. Sometimes it strays into the more sensational — if and when a lawyer can have sex with a client, for example, or lawyer-assisted corporate fraud — and everyone wakes up. Sometimes it's tedious and trivial, dwelling on issues like a lawyer's responsibility to return telephone calls promptly.

While this chitchat is going on, the legal profession is being undermined by a huge ethical problem that is largely ignored. We lawyers all believe that the justice system is an essential part of a fair and democratic way of government (or so we say). But we also know that the average Canadian cannot afford to use it.

According to Statistics Canada, the 2009 median after-tax income for Canadian families of two or more was $63,800. For senior families, it was $46,800. After-tax income for "unattached individuals" was $25,500. These are medians; there are many Canadians who receive less. With this kind of income, you won't get legal aid (available only to those who are really poor, and of very limited scope anyway), and will almost certainly be denied the *pro bono* legal services that a handful of socially concerned lawyers occasionally offer. If you need a lawyer, you'll have to dig into your own pocket. In the cities, where most Canadians live, even a junior lawyer charges $200 or more for an hour's work. Fees like these are beyond almost everybody's ability to pay. The result is that the legal profession has become the handmaiden of the powerful — government, corporations and wealthy individuals.

We lawyers have a big problem. Our beliefs cannot be reconciled with what we know. We believe in equal access to justice (or do we?), but we know it doesn't exist (even if we don't admit it). We live in a state of "cognitive dissonance" (Chief Justice Beverley McLachlin recently used this phrase in *S.L. v. Commission scolaire des Chênes*, so I feel comfortable with it). The encyclopedia says, "In a state of dissonance, people may feel surprise, dread, guilt, anger, or embarrassment." But I haven't noticed any surprise, dread, guilt, anger or embarrassment in the legal profession over the access to justice problem.

The access problem doesn't sit by itself. It is bound up in a complex web with other major systemic issues. Here are some of them. (1) In the modern age, most lawyers see the practice of law as a business rather than a profession; the Holy Grail is profit. (2) Billing by the hour, with its hideous incentives, fuels the flames of greed. (3) Self-regulation by lawyers has proven disastrously inadequate (it has been abandoned in the United Kingdom as part of the admirable and sweeping Clementi reforms of the legal profession and the provision of legal services).

In Canada — quiet, patient, self-satisfied Canada — most lawyers look the other way when the access issue comes into view. But not everyone does, and it's interesting to see who is worried. Chief Justice McLachlin has frequently spoken about the problem. Recently she has cited the World Justice Institute's study that ranks Canada ninth out of the 12 European or American nations surveyed on access to civil justice. David Johnston, the Governor General and a lawyer himself, gave a hard-hitting speech at the 2011 annual meeting of the Canadian Bar Association (CBA) in Halifax. He said, "For many today, the law is not accessible, save for large corporations and desperate people at the low end of the income scale charged with serious criminal offences. We must engage our most innovative thinking to redefine professionalism and regain our focus on serving the public."

In Halifax, the Governor General suggested simplifying legal procedures, avoiding the tort law morass of U.S. law, unbundling activities which do not require legal professionals, and moving the industry standard for *pro bono* work from the current rate of less than three per cent to ten per cent. These are all good ideas, but by themselves they are not enough, and I do not detect any appetite for them in the legal profession. (I wasn't at the CBA Halifax meeting, but I'm willing to bet that everyone politely applauded the Governor General's speech and then promptly forgot everything he had to say.)

Some time ago, in these pages, I proposed a publicly funded universal legal insurance programme. That, I think, would solve the problem, but no one seems the slightest bit interested. It wouldn't be easy to implement "judicare," and to do so would be controversial, just like the establishment a half-century ago of the now-cherished medicare system, which was initially thought unworkable and was fought bitterly by many doctors. We'd have to solve tricky questions, like making sure the programme was independent of government and uniform across the country, and determining its scope. These are not easy matters, but they can be figured out.

Absent something like judicare, well, as someone once said, "Justice is open to all, like the Ritz Hotel." Contrast what Tommy Douglas wrote in *The Making of a Socialist*: "I came to believe that … people should be able to get whatever health services they require irrespective of their individual capacity to pay."

So that's what I decided to talk about in Regina. The biggest ethical problem for lawyers of them all. The fact that most Canadians cannot use the law and legal system that we once thought belonged to all who live in this country.

I'm writing this a few days before I get on the plane. I wonder what sort of reception I'll get.

THE DEBATE OVER LAW FIRM OWNERSHIP
DECEMBER 2011

"It is always a loss not to discuss serious proposals for change in the justice system. It is doubly a loss when these proposals might improve access to legal services." In October 2011 England began allowing individuals and companies outside the legal profession to own law firms, with the goal of making legal services more affordable. The Canadian legal profession has avoided the whole debate.

Is there an ethical reason why non-lawyers should be prevented from investing in a law firm, even owning it outright? Is there ethical danger if a lawyer selling his services to the general public is employed by a non-lawyer?

I don't think there's a problem with these arrangements, but some members of the legal profession disagree. They fear that lawyers working for non-lawyers would lead to a loss of professionalism and collapse of standards. They ignore (or dispute) the access to justice benefits that might accrue to a general public deprived of adequate legal services.

One problem with the discussion is that several different possibilities are jumbled together in a confusing way. Are multidisciplinary practices okay? (That's where lawyers are in partnership with non-legal professionals, typically accountants.) Should law firms be allowed to go public, i.e., sell shares to any member of the public who wants to buy them? Is it a good idea to let lawyers employed by a corporation, say a supermarket chain, offer their services to the public? ("Get your legal advice in aisle 3, next to the frozen lamb chops...")

England recently enthusiastically sorted out these issues. Sir David Clementi, a distinguished businessman, was asked by the British government to review regulation of the legal profession in England and Wales. One of the recommendations in his 2004 report was that companies or individuals outside the legal profession be allowed to own and manage a law practice. The new U.K. *Legal Services Act*, which came into effect this past October, adopted the idea and allows law firms to operate within so-called "Alternative Business Structures" or ABS's. ABS's include flotation on the stock exchange and the "Tesco law" (named after the big U.K. supermarket chain) which allows non-lawyers to hire lawyers to sell legal advice to the public. The Clementi reforms also permit multi-disciplinary practices.

In Australia, this is old news. Multidisciplinary practices have been allowed in New South Wales, the principal Australian jurisdiction, since 1994; now all the Australian states permit them. In 2007, Slater & Gordon, a middle-rank firm specializing in personal injury litigation, was listed on the Australian Stock Exchange, the first law firm in the world to become a public company (the current Australian prime minister, Julia Gillard, was once an S&G partner). This was made possible by the New South Wales' *Legal Profession (Incorporated Legal Practices) Act*, which came into force in 2001. Another Australian law firm, Integrated Legal Holdings, has since followed suit, and no doubt more will be along. Curiously, the largest investor in Slater & Gordon appears to be Calgary-based Mawer Global Equity Fund, whose president, Michael Mezei, used to be a Toronto corporate lawyer. Since Slater & Gordon was listed on the stock exchange, its revenue has more than tripled.

In the United States, the American Bar Association (ABA) has rejected out-of-hand law firms becoming publicly traded and has also kiboshed the concept of multidisciplinary practices. This position was recently restated in a December 2011 draft paper released by the ABA Commission on Ethics.

It is not clear what is behind the ABA's puzzling and retrograde stance. Some American lawyers apparently worry about non-lawyer equity holders pushing lawyers to chase profits at the expense of sound professional conduct. They worry about solicitor-client confidentiality. They fret about lawyers being beholden to investors, and the interests of shareholders eclipsing those of clients. Those on the other side of the debate point out that lawyers have never been shy about pursuing profit. They suggest that removing ownership from lawyers might distance them from business pressures. And, most importantly, they predict that new sources of capital would permit substantial investment by law firms in innovative technology. This would make them more efficient and able to offer cheaper rates to clients. Easier access to capital might also better position medium-size firms to challenge emerging international behemoths.

By the way, as a side bar, the shareholder influence argument against equity investment by non-lawyers is disingenuous. Almost every law firm has a revolving line of credit with a financial institution. A big firm may owe the bank many millions of dollars. This is a form of non-lawyer investment in a law firm, and you can be sure that the investor — the lending bank — will make its views known to the borrower if it feels like it.

The Canadian legal profession is somnolent in the face of English and Australian developments and the U.S. debate. Lawyers in this country have either paid no attention to the U.K. Clementi reforms or have regarded them as some sort of alien aberration. They continue to ignore the important and wide-ranging debate in other jurisdictions about alternative business structures.

True, multidisciplinary practices are permitted in Quebec, Ontario and British Columbia, but there are serious restrictions on how they can be structured and what they can do. Otherwise, rules of the various provincial law societies effectively preclude a Canadian Tesco law (or "Loblaw's law," as one wag suggested), public flotation, or just about any type of ABS for the provision of legal services. If pushed on these possibilities, the Canadian legal establishment retreats to vague ethical considerations of the kind mentioned earlier which do not stand up to elementary scrutiny.

It is always a loss not to discuss and analyze serious proposals for change in the justice system. It is doubly a loss when these proposals might improve access to legal services (the Tesco law, for example) and, by creating new sources of capital, make the Canadian legal profession innovative and efficient and able to offer its service more cheaply (access to justice again).

One of these days something will jolt the Canadian legal profession out of its unwise complacency. Perhaps Slater & Gordon will expand into Canada. Maybe Norton Rose, the U.K.-based firm that has swallowed up Ogilvy Renault and McLeod Dixon in Canada, will become a public company quoted on the London Stock Exchange. Then, the Canadian hand will be forced.

CHAMPERTY
DECEMBER 2010

"It's time to embrace champerty with enthusiasm, 'improper motives' and all." With legal services becoming more and more unaffordable for more and more Canadians, it's time to reconsider the legal profession's traditional prohibition against champerty, the outside financing of lawsuits.

Champerty. It's a nasty sounding word. It means financing someone else's lawsuit for improper motives (whatever that means) in exchange for some of the proceeds. The related doctrine of maintenance means interfering in a lawsuit in some way other than financially. Nice people don't do champerty (or maintenance). Upstanding lawyers don't get involved. It's not ethical. So some would say.

In Canada, champerty is illegal, although the law is, guess what, complicated and increasingly uncertain. In Ontario champerty is unlawful by statute (*The Champerty Act*, passed in 1897 and not touched since), and in the other provinces by common law (champerty is considered a tort). A champertous contract — an agreement to finance a lawsuit — is most likely unenforceable. The prohibition of champerty, designed originally to guard against bad (i.e., rich and powerful) people meddling with the justice system, has eroded somewhat in recent times, particularly since the courts decided that contingency fees charged by lawyers (a form of investor financing) are okay. Some Canadian investors have lately stuck a toe in the litigation financing waters. But negative attitudes about champerty linger on and legal problems with it remain.

It's time to embrace champerty with enthusiasm, "improper motives" and all. Access to justice is the gravest problem facing the legal system. Everyone says so, including the Chief Justice of Canada, Beverley McLachlin (she says so repeatedly). A big part of the access problem is the expense of hiring lawyers and pursuing a claim. Crippling costs put the legal system beyond the reach of all but the rich. Why would we, for some obscure ethical reason, turn our back on a source of financing? How hypocritical is it for the legal system to make itself prohibitively expensive and then deny would-be participants money that could be available to them?

One way to finance litigation is to borrow money. In the United States, third party lending to litigants has become widely accepted. Binyamin Appelbaum recently reported in *The New York Times*, "Large banks, hedge funds and private investors hungry for new and lucrative opportunities are bankrolling other people's lawsuits, pumping hundreds of millions of dollars into medical malpractice claims, divorce battles and class actions against corporation..." One hedge fund, for example, lent money to a lawyer who represented the parents of a baby brain-damaged at birth so that medical and other experts could be hired to testify at the trial (the suit was successful). Lawsuits brought by Ground Zero workers were financed indirectly by Citigroup.

Niches have developed within U.S. litigation lending. One is divorce financing. In Los Angeles, a company called Balance Point Divorce Funding helps women who have no jobs, are raising small children, and have wealthy husbands who are self-employed making financial information hard to come by. Balance Point takes a percentage of "winnings." (It is unclear what happens if there aren't any winnings.)

Appelbaum writes that this kind of lending "is helping to ensure that cases are decided by merit rather than resources." But, that is not to say there is no risk of abuse. Loans for litigation carry high interest rates, and sometimes the costs exceed the benefits of winning. There may be financial pressure to resolve cases quickly. And, it is occasionally argued, investors may think it in their interests to whip up lawsuits with little merit (although I don't see why investors would fund litigation unlikely to succeed).

There's equity investing as well. A close relation of champerty is the buying of valid claims where recovery is uncertain. In the Bernie Madoff bankruptcy, traders have been buying claims against the estate approved by the bankruptcy trustee. Many of Madoff's victims are only too happy to sell their claims for 20 or 30 cents on the dollar. They get cash now, instead of hanging on for an uncertain recovery somewhere off in the future. They walk away happy (relatively speaking). There's nothing new, of course, about traders purchasing so-called "distressed securities" including bankruptcy claims at a big discount from face value. This happens in just about every large bankruptcy.

Some hedge funds have decided not to trade in Madoff claims. *The New York Times* quoted one fund executive as saying, "The fraud is just so despicable that we felt that, from a moral perspective, it just didn't make sense for us. There are plenty of other ways to make money in this business." I don't understand why those with claims against the Madoff estate should be denied this kind of recovery just because they are victims of a particularly horrible fraud — quite the reverse should be the case.

Over ten years ago Professor Poonam Puri of Osgoode Hall Law School argued persuasively in the *Osgoode Hall Law Journal* for abolishing the prohibition of champerty and maintenance. She wrote, "the financing of lawsuits by third-party investors will increase access to the civil justice system for individuals who have meritorious claims but who lack the financial resources to pursue them." Another effect of investor financing, Puri pointed out, would be to deter potential wrongdoers from violating the law because of the greater likelihood that they will be sued. These are obviously highly desirable consequences.

Puri recommended abolishing the prohibition against champerty and maintenance over a decade ago, but, as so often happens with arcane and complex issues, politicians were not interested. And so, partly in the name of a misguided and sloppy ethic (champerty is bad), we are still stuck with an archaic doctrine that frustrates desirable public policy. Prohibition of champerty denies access to justice to those who could otherwise have it. Would-be litigation financiers, with considerable difficulty, try and define what they do as something other than champerty. Third party litigation financing is strangled at birth. The sooner all this changes, the better for everyone.

EXTRAORDINARY FEATS IN
THE PURSUIT OF JUSTICE
MAY 2008

"Sometimes, an individual lawyer shows what can be done about the legal professions biggest ethical issue — lack of access to justice — if you care enough." Two cases of remarkable perseverance by lawyers intent on justice for the most vulnerable speak to what can be done if it matters to you.

Sometimes an individual lawyer shows what can be done about the legal profession's biggest ethical issue — lack of access to justice — if you care enough. Recently, I've come across two interesting examples.

A friend gave me a book by Vancouver lawyer Dugald Christie, self-published in 2000. It's called *A Journey Into Justice*. Most of the book is taken up with Christie's account of his 1998 bicycle trip from Vancouver to Ottawa (Christie was 57 at the time). He took the trip so that he could burn his lawyer's robes on the steps of the Supreme Court of Canada. He wanted in this way to protest against poor people's lack of access to justice. Christie's quixotic journey attracted a fair bit of attention, which, of course, was the whole point. He took similar bicycle trips later, and with the same purpose.

Dugald Christie was killed in a traffic accident on July 31, 2006. His bicycle was hit by a minivan on the Trans-Canada Highway, in the hamlet of Iron Bridge, near Sault Ste. Marie. This time he was heading to Newfoundland, where he planned to attend the Canadian Bar Association's (CBA) annual meeting. Christie wanted the CBA to pass a resolution calling on governments to improve access to the justice system. In an official statement, the president of the CBA said that members were saddened by Christie's tragic death. "Dugald was a dedicated fighter for the rights of Canadians who could not access the justice system," said the president. The CBA did not pass the resolution Christie wanted.

I never met Dugald Christie. He was obviously an unusual man, a bit odd perhaps. Is there another onetime top-flight corporate lawyer who has bicycled across Canada in support of the poor? "Not everyone's cup of tea," said the B.C. Supreme Court Chief Justice when he heard about Christie's death (the judge went on to express great respect for Christie).

A Journey Into Justice is strangely moving. Christie's passion burns bright. As he bicycled to Ottawa, struggling to climb steep hills and put up his tent at night, he ruminated on basic issues. "The questions that would never go away were, 'Am I crazy?', 'Is the law really so inaccessible?', 'What, if anything, can be done about it?'" As he flew home after burning his robes, Christie concluded, "The key to law reform is not just to get the poor to lawyers, but to get the lawyers to see the poor."

Dugald Christie mistakenly considered himself a bit of a poet. *A Journey Into Justice* is full of bad poems, but ones that display the same impressive passion as do his legal musings. He writes: "But how to love our lawyers?/They need a special love/For they dare to rule our country/Not from ground but up above!" Or this, from a poem called "The East Wind," written as Christie bicycled across the prairies: "The powers are against me/And against clients back West,/Too poor to fight back/And too weak to protest.../So what should I do/If it gets me down?/I shall keep pedalling on/And burn my gown!"

Christie was not just a quixotic adventurer, given to eccentric gestures and partial to bad poetry. He represented the down-and-out for many years, while living in a basement apartment on an annual income of less than $30,000. He fought against imposition by the B.C. government of a seven per cent tax on legal services on the grounds that it discriminated against poor people and was unconstitutional. He won that case before a chambers judge and then in the B.C. Court of Appeal, but, after he died, the Supreme Court of Canada ruled against him. Said the Court: "General access to legal services is also not a currently recognized aspect of, or a precondition to, the rule of law." Most importantly, Christie founded the Western Canada Society to Access Justice, which organizes the delivery of pro bono legal services. This admirable organization now operates over 60 clinics across British Columbia.

Not everyone who walks the walk is as eccentric and flamboyant. You don't have to jump on a bicycle to promote access to justice. Recently, at Montreal's Blue Metropolis Literary Festival, I debated the distinguished lawyer Richard Pound. The debate was about the ethics and social commitment of the legal profession, and was high-spirited and good-natured (the advance programme announced, to stir up interest, that "sparks will be flying.") Last year, Dick Pound published a book called *Unlucky to the End*, about Janise Gamble, who was implicated in the 1976 murder of a policeman by her psychopathic and abusive husband. It was clear that she had not fired the fatal shot, but she may have been involved in a robbery that preceded the murder. Gamble was convicted of first-degree murder and was given the mandatory sentence of life imprisonment without eligibility for parole until 25 years had been served. A series of appeals were unsuccessful. She was sent to the Kingston Prison for Women. Gamble, a poor woman who had led a wretched life, was now, presumably, to be forgotten for good.

But, as Pound tells the tale, several lawyers thought there had been a miscarriage of justice. In particular, Colin Irving, a prominent Montreal tax practitioner, thought so. In 1982, Irving saw something about the Gamble case on CBC's *The Fifth Estate*, and it bothered him. He thought that Gamble's sentence was based on legislation not in effect at the time of the murder, and that ongoing enforcement of the sentence she was given violated the prohibition against cruel and unusual punishment in the *Charter of Rights and Freedoms*. He wrote to Gamble and offered his services *pro bono*. Thus began six years of often intensive legal work. At the end of 1988, the Supreme Court of

Canada agreed with Irving's argument, and found Gamble eligible for parole. In 1989, she was let out of prison.

Sadly, a few months after being granted parole, Janis Gamble was killed in an automobile accident — hence the title of Dick Pound's book, *Unlucky to the End*. Perhaps the best piece of luck she had in an unlucky life was having Colin Irving on her side.

ODIOUS CRIMES
NOVEMBER 2007

"Lawyers who defend persons accused of odious crimes may get ensnared in dangerous ethical dilemmas. They may come to share their clients' unpopularity. And they may get on the wrong side of politics." Canada has seen its share of hideous crimes, from sensational serial murders to terrorist bombings. In general, the lawyers who defended those accused in these crimes have emerged from the attendant ethical issues more or less unscathed. But the duties of lawyers who defend such clients remain unclear.

Some lawyers willingly, even enthusiastically, defend persons accused of odious crimes. That's a very good thing for our system of justice, but can be a bad thing for the lawyers concerned. They may get ensnared in dangerous ethical dilemmas. They may come to share their clients' unpopularity. And they may get on the wrong side of politics.

One of the most notorious trials in Canadian history demonstrates the kind of ethical dilemma that can confront a defence lawyer. Paul Bernardo was convicted in 1995 of murdering two Ontario schoolgirls. He was represented by Ken Murray, then by John Rosen. By all accounts, Rosen's behaviour was impeccable, and he emerged from the experience with his reputation intact. It was not so easy for Murray, who for 17 months withheld videotapes of

Bernardo's sexual assaults from police. It has never been entirely clear why Murray acted this way. Presumably, he thought it would help his client. Perhaps he intended to try using the tapes at trial to Bernardo's advantage.

Murray was charged with attempting to obstruct justice, but was acquitted. Justice Gravely found Murray's responsibility in the circumstances unclear, and said, "While Murray made only a token effort to find out what his obligations were, had he done careful research he might have remained confused." The Law Society of Upper Canada began disciplinary proceedings against Murray in 1997, but in 2000, after his acquittal, withdrew the complaint and instead appointed a special committee "to devise a proposed rule of conduct to provide guidance to lawyers who may be faced with similar issues in the future." In May 2002, the committee decided that it needed legal advice (a strange decision, since the committee itself was composed of eminent lawyers). I don't believe the committee has been heard from since. Confusion about this particular ethical dilemma — ponderously labeled by the Law Society "a lawyer's duties with respect to physical evidence relevant to a crime" — presumably still reigns.

Robert Shantz represented Clifford Olson, who pleaded guilty in 1983 to the murder of eleven children in British Columbia. In an article in the March 2005 issue of *BC Business*, journalist Sarah Efron quoted Shantz: "If you're defending someone who's a rotten S.O.B., a lawyer gets painted with the same brush. The more heinous the criminal acts are, the more some parts of the public want to lay that on you." Shantz told Efron that his work on the Olson case affected his health and strained his relationship with his family. *The New York Times* has quoted Ronald Kuby, a prominent U.S. criminal defence lawyer, as saying, "I know what happens in these cases. Your colleagues shun you. The public hates you. Your family begins to question what you're doing."

The Canadian public has just endured the trial of Robert Pickton, charged with the first degree murders of six women (at the time of writing, the jury has not rendered its verdict). His trial on a further

20 counts of murder will be heard later.* The gruesome evidence has appalled the nation. One of Pickton's lead lawyers is Peter Ritchie, who commands considerable respect. He has been quoted as saying, "Sometimes lawyers have to defend highly unpleasant causes, but it's not because they want to do those sort of cases." Police are busy investigating hate calls made to Ritchie's office.

When politics are involved, the situation becomes even more fraught, particularly if the lawyer himself has relevant political opinions. A recent U.S. case illustrates this well. In October 1995, Omar Abdel Rahman, a Muslim fundamentalist cleric known as the "blind sheikh," was convicted in New York of conspiring to carry out a terrorist campaign of bombings and assassinations. He was sentenced to life in prison. The blind sheikh's lawyer was Lynne F. Stewart, a grandmother and former librarian, now almost 70 years old. Stewart has been described by *The New York Times* as a "jolly woman," "round-faced with the slightly owlish manner of a high-school art teacher," and someone who likes to take her granddaughter (she has 14 grandchildren) to watch the Mets play at Shea Stadium. The newspaper also reported that Stewart believes "violence and revolution are necessary to wipe out the economic and racial injustices of America's capitalist system." Of the blind sheikh, Stewart said, "He's being framed because of his political and religious teachings."

In 2002, it was alleged that Stewart had smuggled messages from the now imprisoned sheikh to Egyptian terrorist cells. She was charged with providing material support to terrorism and violating federal prison rules. Some commentators said that prosecution of Stewart, decided upon at the highest levels of government, was an attempt to teach a lesson to radical lawyers who took on odious clients. Others argued that Stewart had overstepped the bounds of advocacy, acting out of political belief, and her prosecution was justified. In February 2005, Stewart was convicted by a jury, and in October

---

*In December 2007, Pickton was found guilty on six charges of second degree murder and sentenced to life in prison. Subsequent appeals were dismissed. The additional 20 murder charges were stayed in 2010.

2006, sentenced to 28 months in prison (she is currently free pending appeal.) She has been disbarred.**

So far, Canadian lawyers seem not to have been sullied in this way. The most politically charged trial of recent times was about the 1985 Air India terrorist bombing. In 2005, after proceedings lasting almost two years, Ripudaman Singh Malik and Ajaib Singh Bagri were controversially acquitted in Vancouver on charges of conspiracy and murder. The many defence lawyers in the Air India case emerged unblemished. Now there are the Toronto bomb plot proceedings. In June 2006, 17 people from the Toronto area were charged under the *Anti-terrorism Act* with terrorist-related activities. They are said to be "adherents of a violent ideology inspired by al-Qaeda." Once more, the defence lawyers involved appear to be scrupulously steering away from the politics of the matter. So far, so good.

**In November 2009, an appellate court upheld Stewart's conviction and directed the trial judge to determine whether she should be resentenced to a longer term. Her prison term was lengthened to 10 years. Suffering from cancer, she was granted compassionate release in 2014. Lynne Stewart died in 2017.

MEDICARE FOR THE JUSTICE SYSTEM
OCTOBER 2007

"The government of Ontario should appoint a committee of wise men and women to consider the introduction of public legal insurance." Chief Justice Beverley McLachlin has spoken out repeatedly about the need for greater access to legal services for Canadians of average means. A system of legal insurance, similar to health care insurance, could be the answer.

Access to law is the great ethical issue facing the legal profession. Most Canadians are denied use of law and the legal system. That's because they can't afford the fees charged by lawyers. Economic self-interest of the legal profession stands between the people and justice.

It's not just disaffected cranks or greedy opportunists, easily dismissed in febrile bar association press releases, who point this out. Beverley McLachlin, Chief Justice of Canada, told Toronto's Empire Club on March 8, 2007 that "much more needs to be done if access to justice is to become a reality for ordinary Canadians." She expressed similar sentiments, even more powerfully, in a speech to the August annual meeting of the Canadian Bar Association (CBA). Just a few days before the Empire Club gathering, another chief justice, Roy McMurtry of Ontario, was quoted in the *Toronto Star* as saying that access to justice is the most important issue facing the legal system. And in August, on the occasion of his retirement, Justice Gomery of the Quebec Superior Court made headlines when he courageously described the escalating cost of legal services as an alarming trend putting the justice system out of reach for everyone but the wealthy. Said Justice Gomery: "I don't think the legal profession is giving the proper attention to the problem and it's suicidal, the direction that we're going now."

What is to be done about legal fees and their bad effect on access to justice? One answer given by some lawyers is that the federal government should stop applying the Goods and Services Tax (GST) to lawyers' accounts (this was discussed at the recent CBA annual meeting). Many of those who advocate this solution are admirers of the late Dugald Christie, a Vancouver lawyer who provided legal services to the impoverished and fought against taxes on legal services. Mr. Christie was an exceptional individual, and the motives of his supporters are impeccable. But, eliminating the GST means that the cost of legal services will be reduced, not by lawyers lowering fees, but by government foregoing tax revenue that can be put to good use in the interests of us all. And, anyway, a reduction of six per cent doesn't come close to doing the job.

It's unrealistic — perhaps even unreasonable — to ask lawyers to reduce their fees voluntarily by a substantial amount. First of all, they won't do it; to think otherwise flies in the face of everything we know about human nature. And, second, someone might ask, why should they? Why should lawyers be altruistic in a serious and special way, when no such demand is made of other occupational groups? Why should lawyers pay personally for delivery of justice to all?

We must look elsewhere for a solution to this problem. The history of Canada might be a good place to begin. A half-century ago, Tommy Douglas asked, "Do we think that the best medical care which is available is something to which people are entitled, by virtue of belonging to a civilized community?" In *The Making of a Socialist,* he wrote, "I came to believe that health services should not have a price tag on them, and that people should be able to get whatever health services they require irrespective of their individual capacity to pay." Douglas's answer to the problem of health services was Medicare, today regarded as a defining characteristic of Canada's advanced society. Now there is a new question: Do we think that the best legal services which are available are something to which people are entitled, by virtue of belonging to a civilized community?

If we do, the answer is creation of a publicly funded universal legal insurance programme, the counterpart of Medicare. I'll call it "Legal Access" (and invite someone to come up with a better name).

The creation and architecture of Legal Access will be contentious and complex, requiring much consultation and thought. Many lawyers will bitterly resist its introduction, as many doctors bitterly resisted the introduction of Medicare (to the point of going on strike in Saskatchewan in 1962). Many will say of publicly funded universal legal insurance that it is too difficult, too dangerous — indeed, impossible. And, certainly, there are hard questions to be answered. For example: How do we ensure that the programme is independent of the government of the day? How can we make the scheme uniform across the country? How will it be administered? How will the programme be financed?

The hardest question of all will be determining the scope of Legal Access. Medicare covers almost all medical services; legal insurance will likely be more limited. Voluntary commercial transactions for profit, such as the buying and selling of a business, should probably be outside the scheme. Routine matters — residential real estate transactions and ordinary wills, for example — may not be covered. There would have to be effective screening to exclude frivolous disputes. The exclusion from the programme of certain kinds of legal matters raises the issue of whether all lawyers, regardless of the kind of law they practise, should be required to participate in some way or other. I believe they should. None of this is easy, but it can be figured out. Canadians are good at designing complex institutions to achieve complicated public policy goals.

What is the first step? The government of Ontario should appoint a committee of wise men and women to consider the introduction of public legal insurance. The committee should consult widely and report to the government. Good ideas spread naturally. As Tommy Douglas said in a 1970 speech in Saskatchewan, "They said you couldn't have Medicare — it would interfere with the 'doctor-patient relationship.' But you people in this province demonstrated to Canada that it was possible to have Medicare. Now every province in Canada either has it or is in the process of setting it up."

BIG LAW IN MITCHELLS PLAIN
APRIL 2007

"A destitute and illiterate victim of domestic violence trumps a multi-million dollar merger or acquisition." While South Africa's post-apartheid regime has faced many challenges and many inequities remain to be addressed, a major law firm, Edward Nathan Sonnenberg, is taking extraordinary and non-traditional steps to promote equality. (This column was written from Mitchells Plain, South Africa.)

Lawyers in Canada should take a look at what is happening here in Mitchells Plain, one of South Africa's infamous townships. They might learn a thing or two about access to justice, the greatest ethical issue facing the Canadian legal profession.

Edward Nathan Sonnenberg (known as ENS) is a major South African law firm, which makes it a big legal player on the entire continent. Its clients include some of Africa's most important corporations and large businesses from around the world. Any denizen of Bay Street would be at home in the Cape Town office of ENS, with its spectacular views over the harbour and Table Mountain, sleek and luxurious fittings, and lean and hungry lawyers.

But ENS has another office, quite a different kettle of fish, only 25 kilometres away from its opulent quarters in central Cape Town. This office is in Mitchells Plain, a township of about a million people, most of them "coloured" (South Africa's apartheid government used this word to describe someone of mixed racial descent). Mitchells Plain is a place of raw living, poverty and violence. The view from this ENS office is of poor people on a dusty street, seen through bars put on the window for the protection of those looking out.

The legal services provided by ENS in Mitchells Plain are free to those who qualify (there is a simple financial test). They are provided, not by junior lawyers stuck against their will in Mitchell Plains and ignored by the big guys downtown, but by the big guys themselves. ENS requires each of its lawyers, no matter how senior, to spend a minimum of 32 hours a year providing *pro bono* legal advice. There is a roster system, and when it is your turn, *pro bono* takes precedence over whatever else you're doing. A destitute and illiterate victim of domestic violence trumps a multi-million dollar merger or acquisition.

Taswell Papier had a lot to do with this. Papier, in his midforties, is from Steenberg near Mitchells Plain (just before he was born, his family, designated "coloured" by the government, moved to Steenberg after being evicted from a Cape Town suburb classified "white" under the 1950 *Group Areas Act*). He became a lawyer, practised in Mitchells Plain, and before the dismantling of apartheid in the early 1990s did *pro bono* work for apartheid victims and for members of the military wing of the African National Congress. In the "new" South Africa, Papier became an acting judge, and president of the Cape law society, turning himself into a distinguished and much sought-after attorney. While president of the Cape law society, he introduced a rule that every member had a personal obligation to spend at least 24 hours a year on *pro bono* work.

One of Edward Nathan Sonnenberg's predecessor law firms (ENS was formed in 2006 by the merger of two firms) tried for some time to hire Papier, but he resisted. Perhaps a major corporate law firm, with mostly white partners, didn't feel like a good fit. Eventually, Papier succumbed to the firm's blandishments, but there was an important condition. The firm would have to maintain his office in Mitchell Plains, and use it to provide free legal services to the local population. In 2006, the U.K. publication *Legal Business* named Papier "World Lawyer of the Year," largely on the strength of his Mitchells Plain initiative.

The Mitchells Plain clinic is run by Lourens Ackermann. Ackermann is from a distinguished Afrikaner family, one with excellent "struggle credentials" (this widely-used phrase refers to having been, in the bad old days, actively anti-apartheid and pro-democratic). "We do retail *pro bono* here in Mitchells Plain, whatever comes in off the street," Ackermann says. "We don't do wholesale, the kind of thing intended to affect interpretation of the law, the stuff that gets written up in the newspapers for everyone's greater glory, constitutional litigation for example."

Almost all Ackermann's files deal with the issues and crises of ordinary people — women with partners who are physically abusive, men who default on their maintenance obligations, the fate of a house when the couple who owns it splits up, the drafting of wills, the conveyance of property. In many cases, Ackermann decides that nothing can be done and sends the client on his or her way. "What people who come here want more than anything else is peace of mind," says Ackermann. "They get it from an honest appraisal of their circumstances, even if the news is bad, even if we have to tell them the law is not on their side." When Ackermann decides that the clinic will take on a matter, he assigns it to a lawyer in the Cape Town office and it becomes part of that lawyer's *pro bono* obligations.

The day-to-day work at Mitchell Plains can be dispiriting. Some people who come into the clinic can't explain why they're there or what they want (they often have a tendency to come back, over and over again). Others, it seems, don't tell the truth. Often a startling and important fact, that changes everything, emerges accidentally late in a client's narrative. "You sit here day-after-day listening to the stories, wondering if you're being mislead and manipulated," says Ackermann. "After a while you develop a weary skepticism."

But, says Ackermann, the work of the clinic "shines a little light into a very dark place." Its most dramatic feature is the way it bridges the economic and social divide, the way wealthy and successful lawyers, used to handling complex commercial matters in hushed offices, assume a direct and personal obligation to tackle the mundane crises of disadvantaged people.

I have a question. Why doesn't a big Canadian law firm open up a *pro bono* clinic in a disadvantaged Canadian community, a clinic like the one in Mitchells Plain, here on the tip of the African continent?

TRADITION AND CHANGE

BREAKING THE LOYALTY BARGAIN
APRIL 2014

"In increasingly brutal times, turning a partner into an employee has been replaced by simply kicking him out. It all seems nasty and brutish." In late 2013, a U.S. consultant produced a report describing the new culture at law firms. Partners who are not seen to be pulling their weight are now unceremoniously shown the door, reversing years of tradition.

A few months after I joined a big Bay Street law office, in the early 1980s, a middle-rank partner left for another firm. This event caused a sensation. There was much gnashing of teeth. Partners went into each other's office, closed the door and had conversations of incredulity. There was whispering in the halls. How could he have done it? Had he no loyalty? Didn't he *understand*? Why, no one had quit the firm since that famous incident in 1951…

I didn't know it at the time, of course, but those were the last days of the Old Order. The loyalty bargain still prevailed, but it was on its last legs. You stuck with your partners and the firm, and they stuck with you, except in the most extraordinary of circumstances. You didn't quit to join the competition, and you didn't get pushed out because your book of business was dwindling. The worst that could happen is that the firm might regretfully cut back on your share of partnership profits.

Things have obviously changed, and dramatically. There is so much flitting to and fro today that you need a program to figure out who's on first. A partner who thinks he's undervalued and can make more money with the competition will not hesitate to cross the street. It happens all the time. The other side of the old loyalty bargain, the loyalty of a law firm to its partners, is dead as well. Firms are quite willing to push out partners who — in their eyes — are under producing or otherwise unnecessary. After all, what's sauce for the goose is sauce for the gander.

Last November, ALM, a leading U.S. legal publisher and consulting firm, produced a study called "Up or Out: When Partners Have to Go." It was commissioned by SJL Shannon LLC, a consultancy that gives career advice to lawyers. The report's introduction strikes a gloomy note. It says "right-sizing" of partnerships is on the rise, "cutting out layers of equity and nonequity partners considered to be underperforming or no longer central to the business. Some long-time partners are abruptly shown the door with virtually no warning.... " It tells us (no surprise here) that the biggest reason why partners are laid off or encouraged to leave is the "inability to develop and cultivate new clients or originations or to sustain a book of business." The report quotes Sang Lee, CEO of SJL Shannon: "Recent changes and recent economic events require firm leaders to look through their new-found lens of efficiency and evaluate who makes sense as an employee and who doesn't. Partners, regardless of how and where they grew up, are being told that there simply isn't room for them at the table anymore because law firms are working hard to keep their head above water."

If you're going to get the boot, how will it happen? First off, there may be little if any warning. The ALM study reported that 77 per cent of partners pushed out hear about their performance problems for the first time when they were asked to leave. Ninety-two per cent of them were offered no help. "They're given the message to go elsewhere but they are not effectively or productively or compassionately transitioned out of their firms. Add to that the reality that the volume of partners that need to go elsewhere is surging and you're left with a market that is saturated with disappointed, frustrated and resentful lateral partner candidates who are making hasty and ill-conceived moves borne from panic and financial need."

But that's in the United States, a mean, market-driven country. Surely it's different in kinder, gentler Canada? Maybe it is, at least a little bit. I think that most times, in Canada, a partner has considerable warning he's slated for the axe. He has lots of time to get into a funk, feel embarrassed, hide from his colleagues (who, he is certain, stabbed him in the back — they'll be sorry), get angry, think of a plausible explanation to give the outside world for leaving the firm where he's worked for a long time, polish his résumé, and — yes — look for another job.

Sometimes there's an alternative to outright dismissal. Remember de-equitization? That puts a partner back into the ranks of employees, takes away his equity stake, means that he'll be paid a fixed salary rather than a share of partnership profits, strips him of his vote on partnership matters. A few years ago *The Wall Street Journal* described de-equitization as a "buzz word sweeping Big Law Nation." One blog commented, "Most lawyers set on pursuing careers in elite firms have long focused on one goal: making partner. Now they are adding a second one: staying partner." In the U.S., seven or eight years ago, de-equitization was the flavour of the day, but it has waned as a technique. In increasingly brutal times, turning a partner into an employee has been replaced by simply kicking him out. But in gentlemanly Canada, de-equitization still has a place.

It all seems nasty and brutish. Why are once-valued employees being treated in this callous fashion? It's because the loyalty bargain has been broken. Once partners feel free to cross the street if they think it in their interest to do so, then firms will fire them if they feel like it. Tit for tat. You can't have your cake and eat it too. What else would you expect?

They used to say in law firms, "all our assets go down in the elevator at the end of the day." That's still true. But, these days, not all of them come back up in the elevator the next morning.

WHEN LAW FIRMS FAIL
FEBRUARY 2014

"The collapse of a law firm is always a bad thing for clients. Always. And yet the interests of clients never seem to figure in the decisions that destroy a firm." In early 2014 a prominent Canadian law firm collapsed, seemingly overnight. Clients, employees and the legal community were caught by surprise.

The titillating collapse of Heenan Blaikie has been accompanied by much *schadenfreude*. That was inevitable. But listen up, all you gloating partners in second-tier law firms across the nation, I'd go easy on that *schadenfreude* thing if I were you. What makes you think that Heenan Blaikie is a one off? In these perilous times, you may be next.

I don't have any inside information about what happened at Heenan Blaikie, but it's a good bet that the greed of some partners was the root of the problem. Once, in ancient times, law partners felt a strong commitment to each other. The general principle was "one for all, all for one," not "the devil take the hindmost." Okay, maybe I'm exaggerating a bit, being a little sentimental. Money has always been important. But, in the olden days, if I remember right, it wasn't the only thing that mattered. Loyalty and fellowship counted for something. Now it seems that partners will walk out the door without a twinge of conscience if they calculate that doing so is in their marginal economic interests. They'll walk out even if they destroy a significant firm, with bad consequences for many of their former colleagues and employees, and for their clients and creditors.

Sometimes it's not unvarnished greed that is the driving force, but a sense of injustice on the part of some partners, a feeling that their true worth is not adequately appreciated. When I worked at a big Bay Street law firm, one of the most successful lawyers there said to me, "The trouble with this place is that there's a lot of boxcars and not enough locomotives." (He, of course, considered himself a locomotive, a great big one with a full head of steam and a boiler about to burst.) If you generate more revenue than the guy down the hall, and you think your share of partnership profits doesn't reflect that fact, then in today's environment of individualism, being only human, you will develop a corrosive sense of grievance. It won't be long before you fly the coop.

What about employees? When a law firm collapses, a few will be invited to follow star partners to the Elysian Fields, but most will be cast aside. Many Heenan Blaikie associates and articling students have been thrown out into a treacherous job market. It's even worse for those further down the food chain, paralegals and other support staff. As Heenan Blaikie collapsed, newspapers reported chaotic scenes in soon-to-be-vacated offices as staff milled about, many in tears, not knowing what to do and getting no direction or information from management. (Meanwhile, by the way, the firm's website was still up and proclaiming, "Heenan Blaikie is constantly on the lookout for talented lawyers and professionals who embrace our firm's entrepreneurial vision and corporate values." Apparently "management" hadn't asked anyone to turn out the lights and shut down the website.)

Then there's the clients. One moment a client is comfortable in the knowledge that his legal affairs are in the hands of a stable team that is part of a firm he knows well. The next minute, he is getting frantic calls from the partner responsible for his files, urging him to follow the partner across the street to another firm (what happened to the team?), a firm the client may know nothing about or have reason to dislike. Profuse assurances about continuity and the extraordinary merits of the partner's new home will, of course, be given, but they will ring hollow.

The collapse of a law firm is always a bad thing for clients. Always. It creates uncertainty, discontinuity, delays and anxiety. Rarely does it lead to better legal service and advice. Lawyers will tell you that the clients always come first. And yet the interests of clients never seem to figure in the decisions that destroy a firm.

And let's not forget the creditors. The failed firm's biggest asset will be accounts receivable, almost certainly pledged as security for a bank loan or two. Long term leases, several in the case of a "national firm," will have to be dealt with somehow. There will be little to liquidate for the benefit of small and unsecured creditors. One thing's for sure. When a law firm collapses, a lot of people owed money — many of them small suppliers — will be stiffed.

Most law firms are now limited liability partnerships, and that offers some protection to partners against angry creditors who come up short. But aggressive creditors seeking blood are not without weaponry. They may take a leaf out of the U.S. law firm insolvency playbook and argue that fees from ongoing files taken to a new firm belong to the estate of the failed firm, a so-called "unfinished business claim." The possibility of such a claim makes acquisition of a new star a lot less attractive to the acquiring firm. Another unpleasant fact for failed firm partners is that they will likely to lose their capital contribution, an amount typically in the six figures and usually borrowed.

There's a lot of pain when a law firm falls apart. Some partners lose a comfortable home and have trouble finding another. Many employees are out on the street. Clients suffer. Creditors lose out. None of it has to happen. Who is to blame? Greedy partners, that's who, the self-proclaimed locomotives who are tired of pulling boxcars and are looking for more money. They have a lot to answer for. They hurt a lot of people. It's an ethical disaster, a fiduciary fiasco.

But there may be poetic justice. Those responsible for the collapse of a law firm may lose more than they gain. Someone once said, "He who is not contented with what he has, would not be contented with what he would like to have." It was Socrates.

BILLING BY THE HOUR: A DANGEROUS TRAP
APRIL 2013

"Why do clients put up with a silly system that leads to their being overcharged and underserved?" In 2013 the world's largest law firm was embroiled in a lawsuit with a former client who accused the firm of grossly over charging for its services. Much of the case revolved around the practice by law firms of billing by the hour.

"Churn that bill, baby!"

That was the message in an email sent by one DLA Piper associate to another about a file they were working on together. The email also referred to "random people working full time on random research projects…" and concluded, "That bill shall know no limits." Another internal firm email, about the same file, commented, "I hear we are already 200k over our estimate — that's Team DLA Piper!"

DLA Piper is not some outlier. It's the world's largest law firm, with 4,200 lawyers in about 30 countries and annual revenues of over $2 billion. The firm has reported that in 2011 the *average* billable hours worked by an associate was 1,831. How much bill churning — baby! — was needed to get to that number? Recently, DLA Piper's complement has shrunk slightly. The lawyers who wrote the emails in question "are no longer with the firm."

The egregious comments on billing were disclosed in pre-trial document discovery for a fee dispute between DLA Piper and a former client called Adam Victor. DLA Piper claimed $675,000 in unpaid bills from Mr. Victor. He said the firm had engaged in a "sweeping practice of overbilling" and asked for $22.5 million in punitive damages. The dispute was quietly settled in April after *The New York Times* started writing about it, and the commentariat, ladling out large dollops of sarcasm and *schadenfreude*, sprang into action. DLA Piper's position was that the emails were "an offensive and inexcusable effort at humour, but in no way reflect actual excessive billing." The firm said it was unfortunate that what happened "distracted attention away from the fact that a client refused to pay his bills."

What the DLA Piper affair reminds us, as if we needed reminding, is that billing by the hour is an absurd way to charge for professional services. I have written before (in *Lawyers Gone Bad*) that billing by the hour rewards, not imagination and efficiency, but the lead foot and the heavy hand. I wrote in that book that it is "absurd to value the work of an intelligent, well-educated person, and especially someone who is creative, according to how much time he or she spends doing that work. On that basis, sudden insight, however brilliant, has little or no value, while laboriously produced hackwork is worth a lot… This approach would value a painting by Picasso according to how long it had taken him to paint it."

Billing by the hour also creates a dangerous ethical trap. It encourages a lawyer to act contrary to his client's interests, most obviously by taking more time than is necessary or prudent to complete a legal task. *The New York Times* reports that in a 2007 survey of about 250 lawyers, "more than half acknowledged that the prospect of billing extra time influenced their decision to perform pointless assignments…" Steven J. Harper, who has just published *The Lawyer Bubble: A Profession in Crisis*, has noted recently that "fatigue through overwork can produce negative returns — the critical document missed during a late-night marathon review; the error in the draft of a corporate filing that goes unnoticed." Billing by the hour encourages sub-standard work and inflated bills.

Worst of all, there is billing-by-the-hour's big and dirty secret. Some lawyers cheat (that's a polite word for it). They "exaggerate" the number of hours worked. They do so in an attempt to increase income, or to impress superiors by meeting billing targets. All lawyers know that this happens all the time, although, needless to say, most deny it vociferously. Deniability is important when it comes to cheating.

What is remarkable about billing by the hour is the absence of serious pushback by clients. Why do they put up with a silly system that leads to their being overcharged and underserved? It's because the only real alternative to paying by the hour is making a subjective judgment about the value of the legal services received. That's a difficult thing to do. It's easier and safer to assess a legal bill arithmetically, just checking the multiplication of hours by rates. If simple multiplication is the accepted method, and the multiplication is correct, then who can complain? But if delicate judgment about the worth of services is required, why, your judgment could be called into question; you might be second-guessed; there could be a lot of trouble.

Imagine you are a middle-ranking lawyer in the office of a large corporation's general counsel. You were in charge of an important transaction and hired the (mythical) Bay Street law firm colossus of Dibbet & Dibbet, known as "Dibbets," to help. One day the Dibbets bill arrives. It's big. It's very big. It's much bigger than you expected. It takes your breath away. Your boss, the general counsel, is not going to be happy. His boss, the CEO, isn't going like it either. How to explain?

The easiest way to justify the huge Dibbets bill is to agree with the multiplicand, the hourly rate, and accept the multiplier, the number of hours worked. Hourly rates are normally set (read increased) annually and tacitly or expressly approved by clients without much fuss. That leaves the multiplier. If you believe the number of hours Dibbets claim to have worked, that's the end of the matter. The bill is okay and should be paid. All is well. Whew!

As I say, it's a lousy way of doing things, easily leading to unethical behaviour — indeed, promoting it. But it seems that the only thing that could subvert the billing-by-the hour system is a general disbelief in lawyers' claims about the number of hours they have worked. Once disbelief becomes general, it's all over. That would be a good thing. Thank you, DLA Piper, for your modest contribution to this desirable outcome.

A CHILL WIND
FEBRUARY 2013

"Amazingly, in the face of devastating facts, new law schools are still opening up." As recent trends have shown, joining the legal profession is no longer a safe bet when it comes to the promise of a long and lucrative career. So, what happens when the once rich pickings for lawyers become slim?

There's a chill wind blowing north, blowing in from the United States of America. In the U.S., lawyers, law firms and law schools are finding the pickings getting slimmer and the auguries becoming ominous. Can our country, tied so closely to the United States, be far behind? What will hard times do to the Canadian legal profession?

The news from the U.S. is pretty much all bad. *The New York Times* recently commented that the American legal profession is "faced with profound and seemingly irreversible shifts." *The Wall Street Journal* reports that applications to U.S. law schools are down almost 50 per cent to an estimated 54,000 this year from 100,000 in 2004; little wonder, says the newspaper, since "barely 65 per cent of 2011 graduates had landed law-related employment within nine months of graduation…" According to *The Atlantic* magazine, median pay for new graduates in private practice has fallen 18 per cent since 2010. Citi Private Bank tells us that the demand for high-end corporate legal services in the United States has fallen about 0.4 per cent every year since 2008, and that during this period the growth in rates, billable hours, and revenue has dramatically slowed. The title of a January article in *The American Lawyer Daily* sums it all up: "The Boom Years Are Not Coming Back, Get Used To It."

The situation, as usual, is more opaque in Canada. We always seem to have less information than Americans, who are well served by a tradition of institutional transparency and by prying journalists who won't take no for an answer. But it would be wishful thinking to believe that the Canadian legal profession is immune to the devastating trends south of the border. Already, between ten and 15 per cent of Canadian law school graduates cannot find articling positions. The Canadian Law School Admission Council reports that this year the number of applicants to Canadian law schools has decreased by four per cent. And according to *Canadian Lawyer*'s 2012 Compensation Survey, the median salary of a first-year associate in 2012 was $72,500, down by approximately $3,500 from 2011. The Survey also found that in 2012 newly called in-house counsel had a median salary of $7,500 less than in 2011.

There's an old saw in the legal profession: a profitable partnership is a happy one, whereas an unprofitable partnership is never content. The maxim applies to all parts of the profession. So long as there is a lot of money sloshing about, and some of it is sloshing your way, you won't make trouble. So long as applicants clamour to get into law schools, professors will slumber on in peace. So long as there is an articling job for everyone, the barricades will remain unmanned. So long as all is financially well in the practicing profession, niceness will prevail. But what happens when law school applications dwindle, articling jobs disappear, and growth slows? Then, nastiness has a tendency to crowd out niceness

Much has been written and said about what happens to ethics in a time of crisis. Some argue that in a time of difficulty there will be an increase in ethical sensitivity, as people realize that strict codes of civility may be all that stand between them and calamity. Others predict disaster. These Jeremiahs talk glumly about what is to come, and may, in passing, mention *The Lord of the Flies* or *The Hunger Games*. As one character says in *The Lord of the Flies*, "Maybe there is a beast.... maybe it's only us."

How might the beast reveal itself as things deteriorate? Denial of the facts, and sometimes outright deception, coupled with flamboyant rhetoric, is one way to rage against the dying of the light. So, Dean Lawrence Mitchell of Case Western Reserve's law school in Cleveland recently wrote, "hysteria has masked some important realities and created an environment in which some of the brightest potential lawyers are, largely irrationally, forgoing the possibility of a rich, rewarding and, yes, profitable, career." In contrast, Dean John Farmer of the Rutgers School of Law in Newark made a confession. Some law schools, he wrote in *The New York Times*, "have been misleading, or even fraudulent, in reporting admissions and employment data." As it happens, Dean Farmer's school was one of them. Rutgers-Newark used to report 90-plus percent employment rates for the newest graduates. Starting in 2012, the American Bar Association (ABA) required schools to report which graduates had long-term full-time jobs requiring a legal degree. The new Rutgers-Newark Number was 56 per cent. Amazingly, in the face of the devastating facts, new law schools are still opening up. Since 2000, the ABA has accredited 19 new ones. In Canada, two new law schools are opening, at Thomson Rivers University in B.C. and at Lakehead University.

Articling students and junior lawyers, often burdened with huge debt as a result of escalating law school tuition fees, may be the worst off of all in the new and unpleasant world. For some of them, unable to get a decent job or even an articling position, their legal careers seem almost over before they have properly begun. Who could not forgive them a certain bitterness, a lack of civility? Who would be surprised if they turned against the traditional professional institutions?

And what about supposedly well-established members of the profession? They're not safe. At a recent dinner, I sat next to a senior partner of a large firm. He told me how his firm has embraced the "corporate model." In the last while, he said, the "CEO" had fired a lot of partners — a lot — who weren't considered productive enough.

As the T-shirt says, "I have seen the future and you're not in it."

MENTORING

DECEMBER 2012

"Helping articling students and junior lawyers get off to a good start is a bedrock obligation of the profession. Nothing is more important." In November 2012 the Law Society of Upper Canada approved an alternative to the legal profession's traditional articling requirements to deal with the rising number of law students unable to find an articling position with a law firm. The alternative offers course work and a co-operative work placement.

Even the brightest law school graduate will likely find himself adrift when he starts to practise his new profession. He may have got a bunch of A's in law school — he may have been a whiz at torts and know the *Charter of Rights* upside down and backwards — but he won't be the slightest bit prepared for the demands and drudgery of daily law practice. The first day on the job can be quite a shock to someone used to thinking of himself as highly competent and super-smart.

Helping articling students and junior lawyers get off to a good start is a bedrock ethical obligation of the profession. Doing so contributes to the integrity of the justice system and protects the profession's future as a respected and important contributor to the well being of society. Nothing is more important. Almost all lawyers would agree with this sentiment, but many do not contribute to its realization.

In part that's because the mentoring thing is not easy. The care and feeding of lawyers starting out, just like bringing up children, is a big job. A legal tyro doesn't ease the workload of his supervising lawyer; he increases it. Proper guidance of an articling student or junior lawyer requires endless explanation of the law, heart-to-heart conversations about anything and everything, marking up memos and correcting draft documents, taking the junior to court appearances or client meetings (and maybe lunch), introducing the idea of law as a business as well as a profession, helping resolve complex ethical issues that sometimes arise — and that's just the half of it. Understandably enough, some lawyers recoil from taking on these burdens.

If you do assume the burdens, you'll pay for it in more ways than one. It's not just the aggravation. There's a dollar cost. The time you spend mentoring is not legitimately billable — it's properly part of your practice's overhead — and it goes without saying that very few clients are prepared to pay for the hours put in by the young lawyer who's learning what to do. I've noticed in the past that in big firms the job of supervising beginners generally falls to those with only a few years under their belt; the most senior lawyers are too busy and important to bother with it, and their time (read hourly rate) is too valuable to be spent this way.

Big firms, of course, can deal with this effectively if they feel so inclined. They have a lot of manpower, and there's always someone willing to take a beginner under his wing (although some lawyers do this a lot better than others). It's quite different in a small firm, or a solo practice, where resources are thin. Then, there is a powerful temptation to let the articling student or first-year lawyer sink or swim by himself — indeed, even worse, to assign him legal tasks beyond his competence. In some cases, this trial by fire might be the making of the budding lawyer, encouraging resourcefulness and instilling independence. In others, disaster results, with files bungled and legal development stillborn. The simplest thing for a small firm or solo practitioner is not to take on an articling student or very junior lawyer, and the statistics show this is what happens more often that not.

And then there is the increasing problem of law graduates who can't get an articling position at all. In Ontario, as many as 15 per cent of those leaving law school are stranded in this way. How are they to be helped to develop as professionals? What are they supposed to do? The Law Society of Upper Canada's recent solution to the problem is a very bad idea. In November, the society approved an alternative to articling called the "Law Practice Program" (LPP). Details of the pilot program are sketchy, but there will be some kind of course lasting four months, followed by a four-month co-operative work placement. Implementation of the scheme will be contracted out to a third party provider; the law society says it does not have the expertise to structure and run such a program, an odd admission by the regulatory body charged with deciding the qualifications needed for admission to the bar.

Critics of the LPP — and there are many — quickly pointed out that those who go into the program because they can't get an articling job will inevitably be branded as second-class lawyers. Furthermore, there are no quality assurances for the LPP educational component, to be offered by an as yet unidentified third party provider, or for the vaguely conceived apprenticeship that will follow. Finally, chances are that the work placement will be unpaid, adding yet more financial strain for a law graduate likely already laden with debt. The cobbled-together LPP program forsakes the profession's fundamental ethical obligations to train and support equally and properly *all* young lawyers beginning their careers.

True enough that there is a scattering of lawyer mentorship programs in Canada. Most provincial bar associations have one of some kind. The Ontario bar, for example, has a "Practice Management Helpline," and something called the Practice Mentoring Initiative which "connects lawyers with experienced practitioners in relevant areas of law to help them deal with a complex substantive legal issue or a specific procedural issue outside of the… Practice Management Helpline mandate." There are various informal mentorship initiatives here and there, and big firms generally advertise some kind of program. But all these are not much more than "call a friend" schemes.

True mentoring, in the biggest sense of the word, is an essential ethical obligation of the legal profession. There is no substitute for the experience of Telemachus in Homer's Odyssey, who received crucial advice from his trusted adviser and guide, whose name was Mentor.

WHO'S WATCHING THE LAWYERS?
FEBRUARY 2011

"Since when is it a good idea for people to sit in judgment of their own kind?" In October 2010 the Legal Ombudsman for England and Wales began operations, part of the British decision to remove the regulation of the legal profession from the legal profession itself.

Someone's unhappy with his erstwhile lawyer. Perhaps the unhappy person thinks the lawyer's behaviour has been unethical. Or maybe he believes the lawyer has been incompetent at his expense. Where can he take his complaint? What satisfaction is he likely to get?

Bring the problem to us, the provincial law society or bar association says. It's our job to consider complaints and mete out discipline. But, the objections to this approach are many and widely recognized. For starters, since when is it a good idea for people to sit in judgment on their own kind? It looks unfair, and that's because it is unfair. And, anyway, many observers (I'm one of them) think the history of self-discipline by lawyers in this country is unimpressive, to say the least.

Four years ago I published a book called *Lawyers Gone Bad*. Much of it was about lawyers who behaved improperly (no prize for guessing that), and what happened, or didn't happen, as a result. From the day the book came out, I have been swamped with emails and telephone calls from people who want to tell me unhappy stories about their involvement with the legal profession. Most of my correspondents describe how some lawyer mistreated them. Many tell me how their attempts to complain to the provincial bar association came to nothing. I've received over a thousand such emails since *Lawyers Gone Bad* came out, and — four years later — messages still arrive at the rate of two or three a week. For sure, some of the people who write to me or call me on the telephone are not to be taken seriously, but a lot seem to have substantial and unresolved issues. Sadly, I have to tell them that I can't help, and that I don't know anyone who might offer succor.

There's obviously something missing in the system. We need an institution, independent of the legal profession, where you can take a complaint about a lawyer and have it dealt with quickly, without time-wasting and expensive pomp and circumstance. The Brits have figured this out. In October 2010, the Legal Ombudsman for England and Wales, provided for by the *Legal Services Act of 2007*, opened its doors. The Ombudsman's job is to resolve legal complaints in a fair, independent and informal way. Says its website: "If we decide the service you received was unsatisfactory, we can ask the lawyer and the firm to put it right. ... Once an Ombudsman decision is accepted, we can make sure the lawyer does do what we say is needed."

The Legal Ombudsman can compel a lawyer who has behaved badly to apologize to his client, and can require payment of up to £30,000 compensation for loss suffered, or inconvenience and distress experienced, or for the reasonable cost of putting right an error. If the Ombudsman upholds a complaint against a lawyer, that lawyer must pay a fee. A consumer must complain to his lawyer first, before going to the Legal Ombudsman, and the Ombudsman, thoughtfully, has published a guide about how a lawyer should handle such a complaint.

Adam Sampson, executive head of the new office, expects to receive about 100,000 complaints a year, with at least 20,000 requiring investigation (the office will have a staff of about 350). All complaints, he says, will be resolved within three months of receipt. Sampson is not a lawyer. The legislation requires that the Legal

Ombudsman's chief executive officer, and the Chair of the Office for Legal Complaints (OLC) which oversees the Ombudsman, not be legally trained. This drives home the office's independence from the profession.

Sampson says he will crack down on lawyers who choose profit over good service, and describes as a "scandal" the profession's past inability to deal effectively with complaints. Chair of the OLC, Elizabeth France, has said that lawyers will be on the receiving end of "rough and ready justice." The process, she said, will not be the kind of quasi-judicial process that only lawyers could construct; it will be consumer-friendly, informal and inquisitorial. Stories in the press about the opening of the Ombudsman office have proclaimed "there is a new sheriff in town."

There is, of course, criticism of the new British arrangements. Some consumer groups have complained that the maximum compensation to a client of £30,000 is too low. Other critics have suggested the office's informal procedure may be too much of a good thing: there may be a new sheriff in town, but do we really want frontier justice? But, most interesting of all is the absence of criticism from the legal profession itself. Are British lawyers unable to think of a good reason why the Legal Ombudsman is a bad idea? So it seems.

The British have done a smart thing, and Canadians should follow suit. Each province should create a legal ombudsman that follows the British model. I believe there would be tremendous public support for such a reform. (Canadian lawyers won't be too keen, of course, but, as with the British legal profession, they will find it very hard to object plausibly.) Five provinces are having elections this fall — Newfoundland and Labrador, Prince Edward Island, Manitoba, Ontario and Saskatchewan. The legal ombudsman proposal should be part of the election debate in those provinces. Politicians should pay attention. The idea is a vote getter.

A final note. It is astonishing how much more progressive Britain is than Canada when it comes to reforming legal institutions. Provision for the Legal Ombudsman was not the only change accomplished by the 2007 *Legal Services Act*. That legislation, among other things, established the Legal Services Board, an independent body responsible for overseeing the regulation of lawyers in England and Wales, removing the regulatory role from the profession itself, a reform devoutly to be wished in Canada.

Why is Canada so backward when it comes to regulating the legal profession?

FINAL THOUGHTS

GUIDING PRINCIPLES
JUNE 2016

"In Canada a law faculty is considered a trade school and its denizens single-mindedly look forward to setting up legal shop as soon as possible." What ethical principles should guide them when they start out?

Almost all Canadian law students intend to practise law when they get out of law school. It's different in some other jurisdictions. In Europe, for example, a law degree often leads to government service, or a business career, or a job in journalism. Europeans think the study of the law develops analytical skills that can be put to general use. But in Canada a law faculty is considered a trade school and its denizens single-mindedly look forward to setting up legal shop as soon as possible. They are anxious to graduate with everything they need to begin practicing. One of the things they require, but may not have, is a moral lodestar. If you are entering the practice of law you should believe — you need to believe — in some guiding principles. Without them you're more likely to mess up your life and career.

Pursue justice, not riches. Practising law is about the pursuit of justice. Don't think of the law as a route to riches. If you do pursue money you'll likely fail in the pursuit, so you might as well be high-minded, if only by default. It's less and less true that a law degree leads to a lucrative career, although the myth persists. A story in *The New York Times* this past June noted, "While demand for other white-collar jobs has grown substantially since the start of the recession, law firms and corporations are finding they can make do with far fewer in-house lawyers than before, squeezing those just starting their careers." The article described "the atavistic rage among those who went to law school seeking the upper-middle-class status and security often enjoyed by earlier generations..." And if you are one of the few who succeeds in getting on the wealth track, you will be subject to the billable hour and many other horrible tyrannies. Is it worth it? What will it profit you if you gain the whole world, or at least a BMW 7 series sedan, and forfeit your soul?

Don't work too hard. Eighteen hundred billable hours a year. That's the famous benchmark for legal practice, and many lawyers claim to exceed this number, sometimes (they allege) by hundreds of hours. To bill 1800 hours a year, you've got to work 50 or more hours a week (not every hour is billable — when do you go to the bathroom?) Those who claim to work this hard are either being dishonest, or are leading a truly miserable life. Save in occasional, exceptional circumstances, no one should work more than 40 hours a week. When are you going to work on your model railroad, or make pancakes for the kids?

A New York lawyer once told me about something called the "Wall Street Boomerang," a term used to describe working all night, taking a cab home at 6 A.M., keeping the cab waiting while you had a shower and put on some fresh clothes, and then taking the cab back to the office. He was *proud* of doing this several times a month. For him, the Boomerang exemplified big time law practice. No surprise that he was a boring and obnoxious person.

Be your own person. Canadians are deferential — very deferential — to authority. Civilization and peace depend on appropriate deference to properly constituted authority, but don't take it too far. Don't join the old boys club. Don't unthinkingly accept the voice of experience. Be skeptical of the law society; bar associations are often not forces for good. Be critical of those who present themselves as your elders and betters and expect you to do what they say and think what they think. Senior partners and pillars of the bar, impressed by their own history and *gravitas*, may try to bully you; don't let them. Your new ideas may be better than their old ideas. Your fresh point of view may be better than their stale view of the world.

Follow the rules. Okay, don't join the club, but do obey the rules. Ten years ago I wrote a book about the ironic inclination of some lawyers to break the law. Why did they do that? I suggested various explanations. Misconduct may be a distraction from the grinding boredom that characterizes much of legal practice. It may be a reaction to depression, or a result of overwhelming pessimism. Or perhaps mastery of the rules of law, and the ability to manipulate them, encourages disdain for those rules ("the rules are for others, not for me"). The practise of law can be psychologically perilous. Its practitioners are sometimes surprisingly fragile. Be on your guard. The price of misbehaviour may be great.

Read widely. Law touches on the whole sweep of human experience. The best lawyers have some understanding of some of that experience. No one person can directly experience much. You enlarge what you know and understand by reading — history, biography, philosophy. Sometimes fiction is the best thing to read, because fiction unlocks the human heart unlike anything else. And sometimes fiction directly illuminates problems that bear heavily on the law. For example, how can we know the truth? Rules of evidence and procedure are supposed to help us do that in the courtroom. If you truly want to understand how difficult it is to establish the truth in a courtroom, read *Arthur & George*, a novel by Julian Barnes about the conviction and imprisonment of someone for a crime he did not commit. It will tell you important things that you won't find in a textbook on evidence.

So, to sum it up, be independent, fight for justice, don't expect to get rich, lead a balanced and big life. Am I being a bit pious and preachy? Perhaps. If you don't like my suggestions for guiding principles, formulate some of your own. As your boat leaves the shore, and the wind fills its sails, you'll need something to navigate by, that's for sure.

THE GOOD, THE BAD, AND THE UGLY
FEBRUARY 2016

"In this country there doesn't seem to be the political will or leadership required for much-needed reform. It's depressing." Some problems in the legal profession keep breaking through the chatter. One is the fundamental issue of self-regulation. In England, self-regulation by the legal profession ended in 2007.

I started law school 50 years ago. That's half a century studying, teaching, practising, and writing about the law. God, that sounds awful! But maybe the passage of time has given me, if nothing else, some perspective (cranky old guy?) on legal issues, particularly broad ethical and structural questions that seem never go away. As I look out there, I see the good, the bad, and the ugly.

The good — lawyers protect us from the state. The best thing about the legal profession is the way it can, and sometimes does, protect the individual from the terrifying power of the state. In Canada, the ability of lawyers to safeguard the citizenry from abuse of executive power was enhanced enormously by the 1982 *Charter of Rights and Freedoms.* The *Charter* has been embraced by Canadian lawyers and judges to the country's benefit. I feel good, very good, about that. A special tip of the hat to criminal defence lawyers who are essential to freedom and are often subject to ignorant criticism.

The ugly — lawyers limit access to justice. Sad to say, most Canadians don't benefit as they should from the *Charter*, or any other laws, because they do not have proper access to the legal system. In 2007 I wrote, "Access to law is the great ethical issue facing the legal profession. Most Canadians are denied use of law and the legal system. That's because they can't afford the fees charged by lawyers. Economic self-interest of the legal profession stands between the people and justice." This is as true today as it was then. No significant progress has been made over the last 50 years. Token *pro bono* efforts don't even begin to address the problem.

In the modern age, most lawyers see the practice of law as a business rather than a profession. Billing by the hour, with its hideous incentives, fuels the flames of greed. The answer, I've long contended, is a state system of legal insurance, similar to Medicare, but that idea is going nowhere (although I recall that at one point it looked as if Medicare was going nowhere and now it is a much-treasured part of the Canadian identity).

So where are we? As the man said, "Justice is open to all, like the Ritz Hotel."

The bad — weak self-regulation by the profession. The legal profession has made a mess of self-regulation. For one thing, we've forgotten that lawyers judging other lawyers is contrary to basic precepts of justice; it's a system that should be repudiated. Discipline of lawyers is weak and capricious. Bar associations are widely and justifiably seen as legal trade unions, protecting their own and proceeding opaquely, rather than transparent organizations that promote the public interest. This has been the case throughout my half-century legal career and shows no sign of changing.

The answer? Lawyer regulation should be removed from lawyers and given to a body independent of both the legal profession and the state. Preposterous, you say? Exactly that preposterous thing happened in England in 2007. Since then, the legal profession in England and Wales has been overseen by something called the Legal Services Board, which has a lay majority chaired by a non-lawyer and is accountable, not to the government, but directly to parliament.

The world of English lawyers did not come to an end in 2007. Almost all constituencies — including lawyers themselves — have proclaimed themselves comfortable with the new regime. You'd think such a reform, in a country that has given us much of our law and many of our legal traditions, would have attracted a lot of attention and discussion in Canada. Sadly, that was not the case. The Canadian organized legal profession has continued merrily on its antediluvian way, and the Canadian people and governments have let the profession get away with it.

The ugly — lawyers ignore the consequences of what they do. Lawyers in Canada live in a legal silo. They have a fragmented worldview. They pay little or no attention to the effect of law and legal practice on economic, social and political circumstances. They pretend that their actions (or lack of action) have no consequences. By so doing they ignore a major ethical responsibility. Partly this is the fault of law schools, which stifle imagination and curiosity and persist in training lawyers to be legal technicians and nothing more.

It is widely believed that a central economic, social and political problem of our time is increasing inequality of wealth, with its attendant evils. This belief has become critical to current political debate in democratic countries. Thomas Piketty argued in his now-famous book, *Capital in the Twenty-First Century*, that the rich are getting spectacularly richer. There has never been greater inequality of wealth, with most increases coming from the deployment of capital rather than use of labour.

Many powerful lawyers are handmaidens to rich corporations and individuals. They protect capital and make the rich richer. Without giving it a thought, they exacerbate inequality that is socially debilitating and politically destabilizing. Remember the financial crisis of 2008? Clever and highly paid attorneys on Wall Street (and Bay Street) had a big hand in inventing the fancy pieces of paper — collateralized mortgage obligations and other tools of so-called "financial engineering" — that got us into so much trouble. That's just one example. There are many others.

I wish I could be more upbeat. Sunny ways, and all that. But these are persistent problems in the legal profession that are not even talked about. The profession ignores them out of self-interest. Why don't the citizenry, and our governments, insist on change? That's what happened in England on the issue of self-regulation. In this country there doesn't seem to be the political will or leadership required for much-needed reform. It's depressing.

A FEW HOURS IN THE LIFE OF...

1. AN ALLEN & OVERY ASSOCIATE

"Allen & Overy is facing a battle to win its associates over to a new time recording regime that will push lawyers to record a minimum of 2,200 'office' hours... One July memo states: '...a lot of the reading needed to keep on top of know-how can be done on your journey to/from work or at home.' ...The memo says the firm believes that time has been under-recorded." – The Lawyer, August 18, 2003

Alarm goes off at 5 A.M. Drag myself out of bed. I feel awful, only five hours sleep. Must be in the office by 6:30. I shouldn't be living out here in north London, 45 minutes on the tube from work, and the tube station a ten minute sprint from the flat, that's almost two hours every day, a tenth of potentially billable hours. Tough to do billable time while travelling but the memo says we've got to do it.

When I'm shaving, I suddenly remember a dream I had last night. I think it was about the Amalgamated Foods merger, although it was all very confusing. The dream maybe was two hours long and I'm billing it. I need the hours (only managed 65 billable last week), and anyway it's legitimate, because after the dream the Amalgamated Foods file seemed much clearer to me than before. I cut myself badly while shaving, no band aids in the flat, had to leave for the tube bleeding all over the place, no time for breakfast again, but managed a couple of cigarettes.

It's pouring cats and dogs. By the time I get to the tube station I'm soaked to the skin, not to mention the blood all over my shirt and tie, also the latest issue of the *All England Law Reports* that I was reading as I walked down to the station is soaked and bloody as well, I must try and slip it back into the firm library without anyone seeing. I read the judgment in the "Millennium Dome Madam" case (managed all the juicy bits in the ten minute sprint), that's ten minutes billed on that corporate embezzlement file and that's legitimate too, because, after all, it's all criminal law.

I must figure out a better way of keeping track of the billable time I spend before I get to the office in the morning and the computerized timekeeping kicks in. Scribbling notes on laundry slips and old restaurant bills that happen to be in my jacket pocket doesn't work very well: there must be some kind of electronic gizmo that will do it and the firm should get us all one if it wants us to record every last minute. By the way, I must be careful to get reimbursed for all those restaurant bills.

Tube is jam-packed as usual. Makes it hard to read the book I've got, *Principles of Corporate Finance* by Brealey & Myers, Seventh Edition, it's almost 1100 pages, in fact virtually *impossible* to read in the tube with people pressed tight against you, particularly with my briefcase jammed between my thighs, but I must figure this stuff out if I going to work on big merger deals like Amalgamated Foods and anyway the firm expects it — they don't want you to spend your time in the tube day-dreaming. I can't hang on to the strap in the carriage because I need both hands to hold the book and turn the pages, and pulling into King's Cross station the driver jams on the brakes and I go slamming into some man reading *The Daily Telegraph* and he sees the blood on my shirt and looks at me as if I'm Jack the Ripper. His face is familiar — I think maybe he's the judge who presided over the Millennium Dome Madam case, or maybe it was Lord Black who owns *The Telegraph* but I don't suppose Lord Black rides the tube at six o'clock in the morning or probably ever. Before we get to Canary Wharf I must finish the chapter on how to calculate option values using cumulative standard normal distributions.

I get to the office just after six thirty, and I'm upset to see lots of associates already there. Some look like they've been there all night, rumpled shirts and blouses, hair sticking up, bloodshot eyes, running around the floor holding drafts of agreements, but I know most of them look like that ten minutes after they get in. I turn on my computer and, on the time-tracking system, enter time worked so far today—two hours on the Amalgamated Foods file, ten minutes on the embezzlement thing, 48 minutes (non-billable) reading the corporate finance book. I'm upset about all that non-billable time, because everyone knows that all that really counts around here is billable time.

A message pops up on the computer screen: LOGGED OUT 11:13 P.M. YESTERDAY: LOGGED IN 6:36 A.M. TODAY; TIME ENTERED 2 HOURS 58 MINUTES: TIME UNACCOUNTED FOR SINCE LOGGING OUT – 4 HOURS 25 MINUTES. PLEASE SEE THE MANAGING PARTNER.

2. A PAUL, WEISS PARALEGAL

"A Paul, Weiss partner, Kelley D. Parker, apparently received a subpar order of takeout sushi. So... she asked a paralegal to research local sushi restaurants. The paralegal took to the task aggressively, interviewing lawyers and staff members at the firm, reading online and Zagat Survey reviews, and producing a three-page opus with eight footnotes and two exhibits (two sets of menus). The memo concludes by expressing the hope that Ms. Parker will now be able to choose 'the restaurant from which your dinner will be ordered on a going-forward basis.'" – The New York Times, *October 22, 2003*

Gretta Jones, who just made partner, called me from Conference Room K early this afternoon and told me to come and see her. "Look at this," she said, red in the face, obviously under a lot of stress, pointing to a plate of hardly-touched smoked meat sandwiches on the conference room table. "I just had a lunch meeting with the top guys from International Machine Parts about their IPO. They wanted New York deli, they can't get it anywhere near their head office in Omaha, it's a treat for them, but they wouldn't touch these. They said they get much better smoked meat sandwiches when they meet with the investment bankers at Sullivan & Cromwell. Have we got a memo on deli?"

I tried to remember the latest list of food and restaurant memos prepared by the paralegal department. The firm chairman had given top priority to these memos, and a large group of us had been working overtime on them for months. I had hoped to be assigned fusion cuisine and maybe even Middle Eastern, but they gave me British (that turned out to be surprising — not just roast beef and Yorkshire pudding, but a lot of tasty stuff) and Portuguese (love those grilled sardines). Working on the memos was stressful, out at night a lot, but it was a lot more fun than the old days, when I did boring filings at the Securities and Exchange Commission and things like that.

"I don't think we have much on takeout," I told Gretta. "The chairman said that takeout is not a firm priority at the moment. There's something on pizza of course, chicken, I'm not sure about deli… I have to check."

"There's got to be something on deli, for God's sake this is New York!" screamed Gretta. "I'm not going to lose a client because we haven't researched smoked meat!"

I called the head food paralegal to check if we had anything on deli, and no, nothing yet, although she said the research is underway. "Deli is a big one you know," she said. "It's not just your meats, it's stuffed cabbage, chopped liver, pirogues, noodle kugel, kreplach, knishes, you name it. And do you know how many deli places there are around here? I've never seen a draft memo with so many footnotes."

I hung up the phone. "Nothing final on deli," I told Gretta, "but it's coming." She slumped down in her chair. "What kind of rinky-dink law firm is this anyway," she said.

3. A LINKLATER'S LAWYER

"Olivier Gazay comes from a distinguished line of French lawyers and judges that stretches right back to the 16th century. So when he announced that he was quitting his assistant's post at City giant Linklaters to set up a chain of designer underwear shops, one or two jaws hit the floor... Gazay's colleagues at Linklaters responded warmly to the news of his career change. 'I had a lot of emails from people who said they regretted the fact that they had not left the law to start again...'" – The Lawyer, *August 2003*

It really made me start thinking when I heard that Olivier Gazay, who worked just down the corridor from me, was leaving the firm to open up a chain of underwear shops. Good for him, was my first thought, and I sent him a warm email saying that I really understood what he was doing. As I said in my email, anything would be better than spending all your time moving meaningless bits of paper around just to make the rich get richer.

I'm a bit old to make a big change, and I haven't managed to save much money, but after Olivier left, and things starting going well for him in the designer underwear business (I saw him in a pub one evening and he looked so successful and happy, buying drinks for everyone), I decided I was going to go for it. As someone once said, damn the torpedoes and full speed ahead! But it was hard figuring out just what would replace the law in my life...

I was interested in retail, but I couldn't get very enthusiastic about clothes, not even underclothes, although I briefly toyed with a high-end suspender shops maybe with bowties and expensive socks as well as braces, but it's a crowded field and in the end I just couldn't get up enough enthusiasm for it. A Porsche dealership would have been nice, but I just don't have the capital. I've always liked fine wines and old cheeses, but that kind of thing just wasn't *different* enough. You have to hand it to Gazay, designer underwear was a stroke of genius.

And then it came to me. Baked goods, top-of-the-line baked goods. That's how "Brioche & Croissant LLP" came to be. I've only got one store so far, but it's a start. I've got to be there at 4 A.M. to do the baking — everything is freshly made on the premises — and sometimes the butter delivery is late, and there's a lot of spoilage, but, after all, it's quality of life that really counts, that and the idea that you're making a contribution and not just spinning your wheels.

I'm really pleased I left the law to start again.